WHO'S THERE?

Also by Simon Loftus

Puligny-Montrachet
The Invention of Memory
Anatomy of the Wine Trade
A Pike in the Basement
An Illustrated History of Southwold

WHO'S THERE?

Travels in Place and Time

Simon Loftus

This edition first published in 2024 by Daunt Books
83 Marylebone High Street
London W1U 4QW

1

The Doctrine of Chances and *Palmyra, a lament* first appeared in
Brick, Canada's leading literary journal; *In Search of Juan Garcia*
in the quarterly magazine *World of Fine Wine*; *The Mysteries
of Rayas* in the annual *In Vino Veritas*; *Brief Lives* in the *New
Aldeburgh Anthology*; *Reading Gardner's History* in the *Southwold
Museum Journal* and *A New Suffolk Garland*.

A CIP catalogue record for this title is available
from the British Library.

ISBN 978-1-914198-82-3

Typeset by Marsha Swan

Printed and bound by TJ Books Limited,
Padstow, Cornwall

www.dauntbookspublishing.co.uk

For
Iris and Nina

Contents

PREFACE

'Who's there?'

These traveller's tales were written at various times over the past fifty years. When a date is noted at the end of a piece it records the journey, not the moment of composition. I have invented nothing, but memory weaves its own histories.

Simon Loftus. Bulcamp, 2023

Histories

On the Red Dragon

Oranges, like mysterious glowing globes, hang in clusters of dark leaves above a hedge of roses, and the blood red seeds of a pomegranate glisten in the gashes of its ripening fruit. Behind this hedge rises a classic Tuscan landscape of terraced hills, olive trees and vines. In front, on a pink stage strewn with broken lances, prance gaudy combatants – dressed as if for a tournament.

Paolo Uccello's *Battle of San Romano* was painted around 1440 (a few years after the event itself) to celebrate a minor skirmish in the endless war of city states, between Florence and Siena. Violence is formalised into images of timeless splendour; warfare depicted as a pastime of civilisation. The reality, of course, was otherwise. Gangs of mercenaries roamed the land. Their commanders, the condottieri, were more likely to be soldiers of fortune from England or Switzerland than citizens of the republics and principalities they served. They were unreliable, dangerous and expensive. But Renaissance princes continued to lavish enormous sums on the destructive 'art of war' in the same spirit of rivalry which marked their patronage of the arts of peace. Only vast wealth could underwrite such luxuries.

This wealth was generated by trade and multiplied by banking. Fifteenth-century Italy was the nexus of the Mediterranean as it had been for centuries past; entrepôt of luxuries from the east and moneylender to northern monarchs. Its prosperity seemed unassailable.

Roses and oranges from China, pomegranates from Persia were oriental legacies to Europe from the traders of classical times, who also brought silk, spices and precious stones. The disintegration of the Roman Empire had reduced such trade to a trickle but there was a revival in the thirteenth century. The rise of the Mongol empire restored security to the ancient trade routes from the east and the European appetite for Asiatic luxuries was rekindled by the Crusades. The leading maritime powers of Italy – Venice and Genoa – developed a network of trading posts along the shores of the Black Sea (at the termini of the Silk Roads to Tabriz, Samarkand and China) and in the Eastern Mediterranean, to handle spices from Malacca and India which had been carried by caïque up the Persian Gulf and thence along the Euphrates to Syria. They also traded extensively out of Alexandria, entrepôt for shipments that had risked the more hazardous voyage, across the Indian Ocean and up the Red Sea. Thus came spices, sugar, dyestuffs, cotton and precious stones. Thus, above all, came pepper.

Prized for the flavouring of salted joints of winter meats, pepper was an addictive luxury for medieval Europe, the equivalent of oil from the Gulf in recent times. Demand was insatiable, despite the fact that all spices were enormously expensive – so costly that pepper and cumin were often used as currency in an age which was chronically short of ready cash. A thirteenth-century ancestor of mine leased six homesteads in Yorkshire, each with a bovate (approximately 15 acres) of land, together with a further field of an acre and a half, for an annual rent of seventeen-and-a-half pence and 'a lb of cumin'. The 'peppercorn rent' was far from the token it has become today.

The price of pepper was extortionate due to the enormously long journey from the east, and because everyone en route (most notably the merchants of Venice and Genoa) squeezed huge profits out of their monopoly. Towards the end of the fifteenth century the price rose higher still as the Turks blocked most supplies through Asia Minor – and Europe became increasingly dependent on shipments from Alexandria. Muslim traders were reluctant to barter spices for European goods and insisted for the most part on gold, to which Europe had limited access. All of which was a spur to exploration, particularly for the seafaring nations of the Atlantic coast.

In 1492 a Genoese explorer, Cristoforo Colombo, persuaded the King of Spain to finance a voyage west, in search of the spice islands. He failed in his objective but inadvertently discovered America. The King of Portugal, much cannier, had spent years sending spies and navigators to learn what they could about the coasts of Africa and trade routes to India. In 1497 he decided that the time had come to put this knowledge to the test. He provided Vasco da Gama with ships, supplies, charts and information for an expedition heading south – with the aim of rounding the horn of Africa and reaching India by sea. Despite losing half his men to sickness and having to abandon some of his ships, da Gama eventually returned, bringing a small cargo of spices as a token of his success.

When the news reached Venice, in 1501, it spread like an icy mist through the city. Venetians whose wealth was founded on the spice trade understood at once that the climate had changed, and several banks immediately failed. Within two years the price of pepper in Lisbon had fallen to a fifth of the level in Venice, and a Portuguese cargo of spices had been shipped up the Thames to London.

Portugal's dominance was relatively short-lived, as the Dutch and the English (latecomers but ruthless) established their own joint-stock Companies to exploit the riches of the orient. Exactly a century after that first Portuguese shipment of spices to London, the *Achilles* and *Hercules* (funded by the English East India Company) limped back home after a perilous three-year voyage and landed a huge cargo of pepper on the Thames quayside. Dumped on the London market, it brought a rare commodity within the reach of everyman, but still made a fortune for its owners.

Everyman in Jacobean London meant the groundlings of Shakespeare's Globe, and by a strange turn of fate the third voyage of the East India Company, in 1607, was commanded by a lover of theatre. In his chest on board the *Red Dragon* William Keeling had packed a couple of recently printed

6

quartos – *Richard II* and *Hamlet* – 'to keep my people from idleness and unlawful games or sleep'. On 5 September that year, anchored off the coast of Sierra Leone, his ship's company gave their first performance of *Hamlet*.

Pepper reshaped the world, shifting the focus of Europe from the Mediterranean to the Atlantic, and changed the course of history. But in this brief, unexpected moment it also prompted a question of haunting resonance, as the opening words of Shakespeare's most famous play were spoken on the deck of a ship, in the cool of the morning, to an audience that included the local African king, his multilingual interpreter and two of his courtiers.

'Who's there?'

Death on the Island

I arrived in La Rochelle in the midst of a howling storm, which rattled the windows so violently that all the shutters were closed, making it impossible to see the waves churning over the black rocks below the hotel. Somewhere in that turmoil of wind and water lay the stump of a stone groyne, which is all that now remains of Cardinal Richelieu's famous digue – the extraordinary fortified barricade that he built across the bay during the siege of 1627.

La Rochelle then was the last great Huguenot stronghold in France – a rich and proudly independent city that Richelieu was determined to subdue, as he destroyed the remnants of political and religious nonconformity on behalf of his most Catholic Majesty, Louis XIII. Thus it was that the relief of La Rochelle became, for Protestant Englishmen, a cause for righteous war – combining religious solidarity, hatred of the

French and the opportunity to seize control of a key Atlantic port – but the expedition which resulted was a disaster and thousands of British soldiers perished on the Ile de Ré, a couple of miles off the coast. One of those who died was my ancestor Dudley Loftus, grandson of Adam, the great Archbishop of Dublin.

So the next day, when it was calm, I went exploring. I walked along the ramparts of the old town, peered into court-yards, squinted through the cracks of shutters and browsed in the bookshops for all I could find about the siege of La Rochelle, and the Duke of Buckingham's expedition to relieve it. In one of these I discovered my first treasure, the reprint of a contemporary journal written by a Huguenot member of the town council, markedly sympathetic to the English forces. The book fell open at an entry for 13 September 1627: 'On the said day was brought the certain news that two thousand five hundred Englishmen coming from Ireland had arrived to help the English.'

I also discovered a vast contemporary map of the campaign engraved by Jacques Callot, hanging in the gloomy hall of the local museum. It showed in astonishing detail the course of events on the Ile de Ré, including the terrible retreat across the salt marshes, when so many men were killed. It showed the French troops herding their enemies into a narrow defile closed by a blocked bridge, where most of the Irishmen died.

Ré lies a couple of miles off the Atlantic coast of France, just north of La Rochelle. It is in a sense a man-made island, formed by the draining and dyking of flooded marshes to join the limestone islets of Ars, Loix and Ré itself; a process of reclamation which began with the arrival of Cistercian monks, in the twelfth century. It was the monks who planted vine-yards on the island and banked the marshes to make salt pans, laying the foundations of Ré's economy. Wine and salt brought traders from the nearby mainland and merchants who made long sea voyages to the tiny harbours of Ré from England, the Netherlands and Spain; but the inhabitants of this low, wind-swept place were themselves indifferent seamen, clinging to the coast rather than daring the deeps of the ocean. They harvested *sart* (seaweed and other wrack), which they scraped from the shore with huge rakes, and gathered shellfish and shrimps from the rocky *platin* when the tide was low. The profits from wine and salt enriched the noble landowners (and the middlemen) but most of them lived on the mainland. For the poorest islanders, particularly those who inhabited the bleak marshes of Loix, life was hard. During the worst of the winter storms they lived on a monotonous diet of dried cuttlefish.

Then, when spring arrived, the marshes became perfect breeding grounds for all the biting insects; so much so that the islanders evolved particular forms of clothing to protect themselves and their livestock from the vicious mosquitoes. They dressed their donkeys in trousers and their women wore the *quichenotte*, a long bonnet supposedly designed to shade them from the sun (or from the amorous embraces of the English – *quichenotte* is believed by some to be a corruption of 'kiss not'); but more probably to guard against the insects. And mosquitoes meant malaria – for the 'ague' was endemic on Ré, as in much of the rest of Europe, until the beginning of the twentieth century.

More grievous than any of these adversities were the horrors of war, as Ré became a battleground in the constant struggles between the French and the English, and changed hands more times than anyone could remember, to the ruin of all who lived there. It was not the insignificant place itself that anyone cared about, but its position as a base from which to attack or defend the real prize, La Rochelle.

Thus it was that in July 1627 a vast English fleet arrived off the coast of Ré, led by George Villiers, Duke of Buckingham.

Buckingham had risen to power and fortune because he was beautiful. As a young man he caught the eye of King James and replaced a succession of previous favourites as the King's lover; 'your most humble slave and servant and dog Steenie'. The King, for his part, addressed Buckingham as 'my sweet child and wife'. After James's death, in 1625, Buckingham retained the passionate adoration of the late King's son, Charles I.

Unlike most favourites, Buckingham proved moderately effective at reforming some of the worst corruptions of government while furthering his own interests, but vanity led him to inveigle his royal masters into a series of diplomatic and military disasters. In 1623 he led Prince Charles on a flamboyant visit to the most ritualised court in Europe, to woo 'the King of Spain's daughter' with pretty gifts – only to have their advances scornfully spurned. Buckingham's petulant revenge was to lead a huge expedition to Cádiz, hoping to repeat Drake's exploits and 'singe the King of Spain's beard'. It was a shambles. So then, in order 'to extinguish the ignominy of the former service of Cales', Buckingham decided to attack France.

He assembled an armada of ninety ships, 3,000 sailors and an army of 6,000 men, together with their artillery and all the provisions of war. Appearances were deceptive, for the

English navy was in such a poor state that only ten of the ships were Royal vessels and the rest were merchantmen, reluctantly pressed into service. More serious was the morale of the troops, many of whom had served under Buckingham in the disastrous expedition to Cádiz, eighteen months earlier. Few of the professional military commanders had any faith in their impetuous leader, and it was widely believed that the Duke himself was loth to set sail, 'fearing some miserable death', or was reluctant to be 'estranged from his effeminate pleasures here at home'.

I am quoting from an extraordinary account of these events that was written by Colonel William Fleetwood, 'an unfortunate Commander in that untoward service'. Fleetwood's *Unhappy View of the Whole Behaviour of my Lord Duke of Buckingham, at the French Island, called the Isle of Rhee* is a very different version than that conveyed in the official reports to the Privy Council (which hid the shameful failures and embellished minor successes), or subsequent rewritings of history by Buckingham's supporters. This vitriolic pamphlet echoes contemporary French accounts and seems to reflect the view of the troops. Coloured by rumour and written in rage, it has the ring of truth.

Right from the start, if Fleetwood is believed, Buckingham dithered when he should have been resolute, to disastrous effect. On the voyage to Ré he scattered his leaky fleet in futile pursuit of a few merchantmen from Dunkirk, and on arrival at the island he found the enemy well prepared. The first contingents to disembark were taken unawares 'by some Troops of French Horsemen' and badly decimated. It was not until three days later that Buckingham himself and the main body of the English army landed on Ré, by which time the French were ensconced behind the thick walls of their recently built citadel at St Martin, which was 'well Victualled for a lingring Siege'.

They were led by the Marquis de Toiras, a Catholic of fierce resolution, and the English could do little except dig trenches and try to prevent supplies from reaching the fort by sea. Both sides fired spasmodic cannonades, during one of which a freak shot from the citadel flew straight into the mouth of one of the siege guns, exploding it on impact. Buckingham grew impatient with such inconclusive warfare, sent endless messages back to England demanding reinforcements and quarrelled with his officers. By August it was being reported back to Secretary Conway that Councils of War were all but abandoned, 'because the Duke finds them other than he expected or because in this state of affairs there is little use for them. His Excellency is of Lord Conway's disposition, to do all his business on the spur.' Professional commanders such as Sir John Burrrows understood that laying siege to a modern fortress was all about patient vigilance, but were frequently overruled by Buckingham; and Fleetwood claims that the troops came close to mutiny. A few French sloops managed to slip through the English fleet, bringing food to the besieged citadel and taking away some of the most severely sick and wounded. Then it began to rain, to the misery of all.

This was the state of affairs when two and a half thousand troops arrived from Ireland, on 13 September 1627. One of those Irishmen was Dudley Loftus. Like most of the Irish troops he was probably a veteran of the expedition to Cádiz and soon, like most of them, he was dead.

The arrival of the Irish coincided with the intensification of hostilities between the citizens of La Rochelle and their King, as the first shots were fired from the city at the royal troops; but this also meant that Richelieu's army was now in place and able to concentrate some of its efforts on the relief of St Martin. On several occasions in the following month sloops were dispatched to Ré under cover of darkness, in an attempt to slip past the English defences, and a few of them got through.

These supplies were not enough to save the citadel from slow starvation, and the Marquis de Toiras eventually recognised that he might be forced to capitulate. He himself was ill, as were many of his soldiers, and all were hungry; so Toiras began to discuss terms with Buckingham, and agreed to surrender the citadel on 8 November. He chose that date in the faint hope that help might still arrive with the high tide of the full moon, on the night of the seventh, knowing that he could hold out no longer.

As it transpired the moon was indeed full but overcast by clouds, and the night was dark enough for a flotilla carrying food, troops and munitions to sail close inshore and escape the last-minute attempts at interception, when finally spotted by the English. The following morning Buckingham's disconsolate troops (who were also suffering from an acute shortage of food) woke to the sight of their enemies waving joints of meat and loaves of bread, impaled on their pikes.

Fleetwood explains this sudden change in fortune by a lurid tale of treachery and incompetence. In his version of events the main responsibility for maintaining a vigilant siege had been assumed by Sir John Burrows, whose judgement was trusted by the troops; but Buckingham frequently over-ruled his orders and one day, while Sir John was 'surveying the trenches, well out of range of the Fort', he was shot dead. Fleetwood makes it quite clear that he believes Burrows was shot by an agent of the Duke, who shortly thereafter withdrew 'two of the best regiments from the siege to safeguard his own person'. It was as a result of these actions that the French were able to reprovision the garrison.

Whatever the truth of this story, Buckingham's army was now in dire straits; desperately short of food, weakened by sickness (it had rained for weeks) and faced by a reinforced garrison. Several English ships had foundered in the winter storms and the mariners were close to mutiny. To add to their plight, the French had managed to land a force of several thousand troops on the south of the island and were rapidly advancing to attack the English from the rear.

It was at this point, according to Fleetwood, that Buckingham took fright. He lied to his officers, telling them that most of the garrison had covertly withdrawn, and had a common soldier who resembled him dressed in his clothes while he got himself aboard ship, out of harm's way. This fantastic story is almost certainly false, but is just the sort of rumour that can so easily spread in a demoralised army.

Most accounts agree that Buckingham ordered his troops to launch a last, all-out assault on the citadel, encouraged by the mass singing of psalms; but their scaling ladders were too short to reach the top of the walls, the garrison fired down at them with lethal effect and then sallied from their fortress as the English turned and fled. 'Which retreat cost most of us our lives', for the way to safety was over marshy land towards a narrow causeway, and thence by a wooden bridge across a treacherous creek, separating the main part of the island from the northern islet of Loix; off which the English fleet lay anchored. Buckingham had guarded the bridge itself but not the approaches to the causeway, which meant that his army was herded like sheep to the slaughter, harried from the rear by the recently landed French troops and funnelled into a trap, for the bridge was blocked.

In our flight we aimed at a certain narrow bridge, over a great River, which if we could have recovered and passed, we had stopt the pursuit of our Enemies, but through their pollicy we were prevented by their over-turning a loded Cart there beforehand which we must either climbe over, or leape into the River, or Salt-pits, which most of our Company being unable to doe, were instantly hewn in peeces, Sir Charles Rich and others of great esteeme, who in the deadly extremity were offered quarter, but would not, rather chusing to dye honourably, then longer to live with infamy and torment. I my selfe perceiving the folly of resisting any longer, having one of the best Horses in the Company, was forced to take an infirme Salt-pit, where both my selfe and my horse stuck fast in the ground, and where I had suddenly a gashly wound in the legge with a Bullet, and so I lay struggling for Life, Lord, Lord (me thought) what paine it was to dye so, and divers of our Company and Commanders were in like distresse, But in the end the French horsemen, wanting shot to reach us in the water, by the valiancy of the poore remainder of our souldiers, that were gotten over the Cart, wee were dragged a shoare, and so being at that time unpursued, were conveyed out of danger.

Fleetwood's account tallies with that of Sir Pierce Crosby (a commander of the Irish troops) who wrote a letter describing the assault on St Martin and the retreat that followed, including the carnage at the blocked bridge. It seems most likely that Dudley Loftus, as one of those Irishmen, was killed in these marshes by the causeway.

When the English fleet finally reached Portsmouth, they counted the dead. 6,000 troops had embarked in the summer, and 2,000 Irish reinforcements had joined them in September. Less than half returned.

Shame, anger and grief at this disaster brought calls for Buckingham's impeachment. By June 1628 the clamour had mounted to such a point that Parliament issued a formal remonstrance against the King's favourite, demanding his removal from office. Charles angrily prorogued Parliament.

Two months later, on 17 August 1628, the Duke of Buckingham left London for Portsmouth, to take command of a new expedition to La Rochelle. His appointment was an act of astounding arrogance by the King, in the face of widespread outrage, and Buckingham seems to have sensed that fate was against him; his last act before departing was to make his will.

Immediately on arrival at the port the Duke was 'affronted' by a sailor, who 'was by a martiall courte condemned to die; after which the saylers in great multitudes drewe together with cudgels and stones, and assayed with great fury' to release the prisoner. A riot developed, muskets were fired and the mutiny was only ended when Buckingham charged the rioters at the head of a troop of cavalry, swords drawn. The Duke 'himselfe in person sawe the first mutinere carried with a guarde to the gibbet, where he was hanged by the handes of another mutinous sayler, who himselfe was saved for that good office'.

A few days earlier 'a lean man with red hair and dark, melancholy features' had bought a ten-penny knife on Tower Hill and set out to walk the seventy miles to the south coast, in pursuit of his prey. On the night of the 22nd he slept a few miles outside the port and the next morning went to a house in the High Street where Buckingham was lodging. He gained access, being known to the guard, and hid behind a curtain in the hall while the Duke finished his breakfast. 'Having received that morning [the false] news that Rochell was relieved', Buckingham 'was very jocant and well pleased' as he emerged from the dining room. He paused for a moment to greet one of his officers, Colonel Sir Thomas Fryer – whereupon the red-haired man reached over the colonel's shoulder, and 'stabbed the duke above the left pappe, cleane through a rib. The duke, pulling the knife himselfe out cryed out with a great oath, "Traytor, thou hast killed me," and drewe his sworde halfe out, and so fell downe and never spoke worde more. When with a shouting shrike every body withdrewe, and none knewe who killed him.'

The murderer made no attempt to flee but stepped calmly forward as the hubbub mounted and claimed his place in popular myth: 'No villain did it but an honourable man. I am the man.' He raised his voice against the outcry of the crowd. 'In your hearts you rejoice at my deed.'

His name was John Felton. Having served as a lieutenant in the disastrous expedition to Ré, Felton had been promised promotion but this was denied him, and some say his wages had not been paid. Bitterness at being passed over (as others who never risked their lives were preferred in his place) was compounded by a Puritan sense of destiny. Felton had sewn into the lining of his hat a scrap of paper scrawled with a few obscure lines, referring to a sacrifice for the honour of God. 'Lett noe man commend me for doinge of it, but rather discommend themselves as the cause of it, for if God had not taken away our harts for our sinnes he would not have gone so longe unpunished.' Afterwards, when he was questioned, Felton claimed that he had been prompted to his deed by 'reading the remonstrances of the Houses of Parliament' (calling for Buckingham's impeachment) and had become convinced that in 'killing the Duke he should do his country great service'.

That is certainly how the country saw it, for Buckingham's death was greeted with bonfires and celebrations, and his murderer became the toast of England; while King Charles flung himself on his bed, in a storm of tears. It is said that crowds lined the road as Felton was taken to prison, shouting 'the Lord comfort thee', and that an old woman cried out to him as he passed, 'God bless thee, little David.' When the King came to Portsmouth, to witness the departure of the fleet, the crews called out to him to 'spare John Felton, their sometime fellow soldier'. Even the royal masque-maker, Ben Jonson, was hauled before the authorities on suspicion of having written some widely circulated verses, *To His Confined Friend Mr Felton*, and only escaped punishment by vehemently denying what could not be proved. Another contemporary poet celebrated Felton's deed in words that echoed the common mood:

> Live ever Felton, thou hast turned to dust
> Treason, ambition, murther, pride, and lust.

This outburst of popular feeling transformed Felton into a hero, and stories continued to accumulate round his name, for centuries afterwards. Dumas made him an honest dupe, seduced by the wicked Milady de Winter, who bewitched him to murder Buckingham. Another more recent fiction claims him as the Royal Botanist, who went with Buckingham to Ré in order to record the local flora, which he sketched in the midst of war. This version includes the haunting image of Felton being pelted with flowers (in late November) as he made his way to the scaffold.

I love those stories, but the real man seems at least as interesting as his fictional namesakes. John Rushworth, writing thirty years after the event, tells us that Felton was brought before the Privy Council, which 'pressed him to confess who set him to work on such a bloody Act, and if the Puritans had no Hand therein' – and that Dr Laud, Bishop of London, threatened him with the rack. Felton replied with extraordinary boldness, 'that if it must be so he could not tell whom he might nominate in the Extremity of Torture, or which of their Lordships he might name, for Torture might draw unexpected Things from him: after this he was asked no more Questions but sent back to Prison'.

In the months between arrest and execution Felton suffered great remorse and came to accept 'that the common good could in no way be a pretence to a particular mischief'. He even requested that his hand be cut off, as part of his punishment, but the judges refused. He was hanged at Tyburn on 29 November 1628.

Dudley Loftus lies in an unmarked grave, somewhere in the marshes of Ré. Buckingham's corpse was buried in state at Westminster Abbey, in a magnificent tomb next to that of his lover, King James. Felton's body was taken to Portsmouth and hung in chains on a gibbet near the docks, until it rotted.

Heere uninterr'd suspends (though not to save
Surviving friends th'expences of a grave)
Felton's dead earth; which to the world must bee
Its owne sad monument, his elegie;
As large as fame, but whether badd or good
I say not: by himself 'twas writt in blood;
For which his body is entombed in ayre,
Archt o're with heaven, sett with a thousand faire
And glorious diamond starrs. A sepulchre
That time can never ruinate, and where
Th'impartiall worme (which is not brib'd to spare
Princes corrupt in marble) cannot share
His flesh; which if the charitable skies
Embalme with teares; doeing those obsequies
Belong to men: shall last, till pittying fowle
Contend to beare his bodie to his soule.*

---

* *Poems & Songs relating to George Villiers, Duke of Buckingham* (Percy Society, London, 1850).

The Doctrine of Chances

De Moivre (A.)
The Doctrine of Chances,
contemporary calf, rather worn, 4to, 1718
With handwritten inscription on the flyleaf:
*Mr Mollet and Mr Dobby at Backgammon 29 May
1740 under the awning on board His Majesties
Ship Dunkirk Capt. Bolling & Mr Stafford
first Lieutenant looking on.*

It was the title that caught my eye but the accompanying
note that held my attention. I was browsing through a thick
catalogue which summarised the dispersal at auction of the
entire contents of a large country house – grand furniture,
family portraits, photograph albums; silver, china and glass;
children's toys; clothes and miscellaneous junk; and a library
of books which included (beside the usual works on hunting,
shooting and genealogy) the first English edition of Marx's
Capital. This revolutionary time bomb bore the bookplate of
its first owner, Sir Alfred Sherlock Gooch, the 9th Baronet

of that name; a contemporary of Marx whose wealth derived from the inheritance of large tracts of land in the centre of Birmingham but who preferred to live on his vast estates in Suffolk, far removed from the taint of commerce. I found the two faded volumes of *Capital* sitting on the bookshelves close to the leather-bound copy of Abraham de Moivre's work on mathematical probability, which also belonged to Sir Alfred, and I found myself reconsidering my mental image of this nineteenth-century landowner, whose descendants seem to have forgotten how to read.

De Moivre published *The Doctrine of Chances* in 1718 and dedicated it to his close friend, Sir Isaac Newton. An elaboration of a much earlier paper, delivered to The Royal Society, it was the first publication in English to deal with the principles of a new branch of mathematics, the theory of probability.

Probability theory was built on strange foundations, by men of genius. It began in 1654 with the correspondence between Blaise Pascal and Pierre de Fermat, in response to a request from an aristocratic gambler – who sought Fermat's help in calculating the odds of being dealt various hands at cards. Pascal had developed Differential Calculus and invented the hydraulic press, while Fermat was a magistrate who dabbled in mathematics for his own amusement. He was one of the founders of Number Theory and teased future generations with his infamous Last Theorem, for which he claimed to have found an elegant solution that he never divulged. Both of them as it happened were fascinated by games of chance and together they evolved the first rudimentary equations of mathematical probability, to improve the odds of winning against less numerate opponents.

A few months after his unpublished correspondence with Fermat, Pascal experienced a religious revelation that led him to abandon mathematics for Jansenist philosophy, but his work was taken up by a Dutchman, the greatest polymath of his age. Christian Huygens was extraordinary; the first man to regulate a clock with a pendulum, he also invented a better telescope and with it found Titan, the largest of Saturn's moons. Huygens discovered polarisation, evolved a wave theory of light (well over a century before this could be proved) and in 1657 published a famous treatise on the odds at dice games, *De Ratiociniis in Ludo Aleae*. All of which should have made this prodigy unbeatable at dice, had his theories not been flawed by his failure to understand the complex probabilities of compound events or to recognise that statistical prediction is only reliable with very large samples.

These were the areas where de Moivre made his most important advances, the reason why his work on gambling (all but forgotten today) is celebrated by mathematical historians. De Moivre had read Huygens' work but disagreed with his conclusions. 'Tho' I have not followed Mr Huygens in his Method of Solution, 'tis with very great pleasure that I acknowledge the Obligations I have to him; his Book having Settled in my Mind the first notions of this Doctrine, and taught me to argue about it with certainty.' He used Huygens' work as a springboard to develop his own theories. De Moivre's 'Doctrine of Combinations' (which was first published to the world in *The Doctrine of Chances*) declared that the probability of a compound event, composed of the intersection of statistically independent circumstances, is the product of the probabilities of its components. This enabled much more accurate calculations, particularly in the field of life insurance. His subsequent discovery of the Central Limit Theorem apparently made it easier to understand what is now called The Weak Law of Large Numbers (that probability calculations work best the more times you throw the dice); but here I get lost in equations of impenetrable obscurity.

De Moivre talked about the pitfalls of a common-sense approach and the need to 'distinguish Truth from what seems so nearly to resemble it' (a lovely phrase), and he illustrated this by calculating the odds of winning at Lotteries – with startling results. I was reminded of the time many years ago when a mathematical friend (tall, short-sighted, suffering the pangs of Irish Catholic guilt and unfulfilled lust) tried to explain to me the rudiments of Probability Theory. The explanation happened late one night, over the dregs of a bottle, and my clearest memory is of Pat Carroll arguing with passionate incoherence that probability enabled him to calculate the odds of a golfer hitting a hole-in-one (his unacknowledged dream) but not to predict the actual successful swing or even to be certain that a bright white golf ball might not pop briskly out of the hole, as he was striding down to the green.

I took this, then, as clear proof of the madness of mathematicians but now, increasingly, I recognise a strange truth in this surreal memory: that the laws of chance cannot prevent the gambler tossing a string of sixes, against the overwhelming odds. Uncertainty is the flipside of probability.

But De Moivre was a Huguenot refugee, with a pure, statistical view of the world – uncertainty was his bête noir, to be chained with algebra. He claimed that 'The Doctrine of Chances may ... help to cure a Kind of Superstition, which has been of long standing in the World, *viz* that there is in Play such a thing as Luck, good or bad.' Croupiers and bookies know that De Moivre was right – that it all boils down to numbers – but gamblers recognise a different truth, that across the broad oceans of probability roll the waves of luck. Waiting for the monster, the mighty wave, they are surfers of chance – playing for the highest stakes as they ride the breaking crest or speed along the inner curve of a falling, liquid wall, far beyond calculation, on the brink of imminent disaster.

De Moivre had arrived in England as a refugee from religious persecution in France but soon became friends with two of the greatest men of his day – Newton and Halley – and was elected a Fellow of the Royal Society. English aversion to foreigners (or his own eccentric nature) somehow prevented those social and scientific connections being translated into what he needed, a post at one of the Universities, and De Moivre was forced to employ his talents for more prosaic purposes – earning a precarious living by tutoring the sons of grandees, calculating the rates for annuities, and gambling. Even as a gambler he was unable to demonstrate that the equations of probability were a sufficient substitute for the waves of luck, which he regarded as an illusion.

This haphazard way of life continued until he was old, when De Moivre was overcome by lethargy, and perhaps by a sense that the odds were against him – for he had long ago decided that the maximum span of human life, statistically speaking, was eighty-six years. Having lost the senses of sight and hearing he spent longer and longer in bed, until eventually he was sleeping for twenty hours at a stretch. His friends joked sadly that there would soon come a time when he slept the whole day through – and so it was. On 27 November 1754, six months after his eighty-seventh birthday, Abraham de Moivre woke no more; but he had in a sense beaten the odds.

What of his masterpiece, *The Doctrine of Chances?* There is nothing gestural about the writing, no sense of leading us through scenes of revelation to the ultimate coup de théâtre, the great Theory of Probability. On the contrary, it is closer in style to a ship's log, reducing the magic of weather and movement, heaving seas and billowing canvas, the smell of the spray and the flight of fish to a series of notations – latitude and longitude, time of day, barometric pressure, the repetitive roster of duty. De Moivre recounts his solutions to the gambling problems set by his friend, Mr Francis Robartes, as sets of equations, series of numbers. And then at the end, for the benefit of those without algebra, he demonstrates the same points again in language comprehensible to numerical idiots. There is little hint, except in the dedication to Newton, that wrestling with chance is anything other than a matter of logic and number, practical stuff – no suggestion that de Moivre recognised the seminal importance of his work. His greatest claim is that he 'fix'd certain Rules, for estimating how far some sort of Events may rather be owing to Design than Chance', and thereby provided 'the Evidence of exquisite Wisdom and Design, which appear in the Phenomena of Nature throughout the Universe'.

Revealing the 'exquisite Wisdom and Design' which underpin the workings of chance is certainly a higher claim than calculating the odds for life insurance, but I prefer a more anarchic view – that chance is the truest expression of an apparently ordered world, that the random miracles of chaos reveal more about the fundamental nature of our universe than the finest constructs of the Age of Reason. Probability Theory needs to be stood on its head so that finally, as my mathematical friend predicted, the golf ball pops out of the hole, in a perfect demonstration of Murphy's Law.

Considerations of this kind pursued me as I researched the circumstances of that tiny moment of social history, on 29 May 1740, when someone was reading *The Doctrine of Chances* on the deck of an English warship, as a couple of friends played backgammon, underneath the awning. This, surely, was a compound event – all the probabilities of which De Moivre could have calculated and then combined, to predict an end result.

I began with the ship. HMS *Dunkirk* was a Fourth Rater (two decks, forty eight guns, 140 men), which had been built at Portsmouth between 1731 and 1734. She was broken up fifteen years later, in 1749. Most of her logs, musters and pay lists survive in the National Archives, in London.

So far, so good; but then the puzzles began. On Thursday 29 May 1740 HMS *Dunkirk* was at sea in the Atlantic, off the Scilly Isles. She travelled 32 miles in 'light airs and hazey weather', which gradually gave way to 'moderate gales and thick weather with some rain'. It was much the same for the rest of that week – grey, 'inclinable to be foggy', somewhat stormy. There was no possibility that the awning could have been spread or that Mr Mollet and Mr Dobby were playing backgammon on deck – even had their names appeared on the ship's muster lists, which they did not. Nor did Captain Bolling, but there was a William Stafford, listed amongst the 'Supernumeraries'; perhaps this was our man.

I checked the inscription again, but the date seemed unambiguous. Then it occurred to me that the Gregorian calendar was not adopted in England until 1752, prior to which the year began on 25 March, and that sometimes I find myself writing last year's date, from force of habit, several weeks after the New Year has begun. It seemed possible that the game of backgammon had actually taken place in May 1741.

The ship's log suggested that I was right. At half past seven in the evening of Friday 29 May 1741 HMS *Dunkirk* 'Came to an anchor in 15 fathoms water with ye best bower [the main bow anchor] . . . Found riding here his Majesty's ship[s] Suffolk, York and Experiment.' The location is recorded as 'Mattalena Harbour'. It is clear from the rest of the log that these British warships were patrolling the north coast of South America, following Admiral Vernon's ill-fated attack on Cartagena earlier that year. You can imagine the quarterdeck awning being spread and the games board opened, as Messrs Mollet and Dobby, Bolling and Stafford caught a breath of the evening air, after another day of humid, oppressive weather, typical of the rainy season in the Caribbean.

But where was Mattalena, a name that appears in none of the gazetteers? The *Dunkirk*'s log omits any map references for the crucial day but it does record her latitude for 27 May as 11°:10'N, and on 30 May her position is shown as 'Lattd 12°:19'N. Long^t 00°:57'W'. The latitudes are consistent with the Caribbean but the longitude seems crazy; nowadays those references would indicate somewhere near the town of Tamale, in northern Ghana. Then I learnt that the Greenwich meridian was not generally adopted as the base line of longitude by the Royal Navy until after 1766, when the Astronomer Royal, the Reverend Nevil Maskelyne, published the first edition of his *Nautical Almanac and Astronomical Ephemeris*. Together with its companion volume, the *Tables Requisite*, this provided a vast improvement on previous methods of calculating longitude, enabling a degree of accuracy which was only surpassed by the gradual adoption of the marine chronometer, invented by Maskelyne's foe, John Harrison. Until these developments longitude was often measured from some local 'zero line', to make calculations easier, and in the case of Admiral Vernon's expedition to Cartagena it seems that the 75th meridian was adopted for this purpose.

Close reading of the *Dunkirk*'s log yielded another clue to her whereabouts. On 28 May she was lying off the easternmost point of 'Galera de Jamba'. No modern map that I consulted showed any such place but an old school atlas, published before the First World War, marked Galera de Zamba bay – north-east up the coast of Colombia from Cartagena. Fifty miles further up that coast was the mouth of the Magdalena River, i.e. 'ye Mouth of Mattalena', as referred to in the entry for 30 May. Now at last I could visualise the broad, swampy estuary where the ship was anchored, when the backgammon game began.

In the eighteenth century the whole of this region of South America (present day Colombia and much of Venezuela) comprised the viceroyalty of New Grenada – The Spanish Main. Gold, tobacco, beans and hides were exported from three fortified harbours – Porto Bello (on the isthmus of Panama), the naval base of Cartagena and Caracas – and slaves were shipped from Africa to work in the mines and plantations. Porto Bello had been attacked with great daring by six ships under Admiral Vernon in 1739, at the start of the so-called 'War of Jenkins' Ear' between England and Spain, and the Admiral was anxious to repeat his success. He was eventually given a chance to do so and arrived in the Caribbean in January 1741, with a vast fleet at his command. According to a near-contemporary (Dr John Campbell) the fleet comprised 'thirty ships of the line, with a considerable number of frigates, bomb-ketches, fire-ships, etc. The number of seamen was about fifteen thousand, and that of the land forces at least twelve thousand, including four battalions raised in America, and five hundred negroes from Jamaica.' This mighty force, 'doubtless the most tremendous that ever appeared in those seas', was completely wasted. A series of unnecessary delays allowed the Spanish to prepare their defences, while the start of the rainy season meant that the British were committed to waging war in particularly unhealthy weather. Delays were compounded by quarrels between Vernon and the military commander, General Wentworth, and by misjudgements at every stage of the campaign. Cartagena was attacked but not taken, casualties were heavy and Vernon's vast fleet eventually retired to Jamaica, leaving a small squadron to cover its departure. Among the ships in that squadron was HMS *Dunkirk*.

'Diseases, peculiar to the climate, raged with inconceivable malignity, and many brave men who had escaped the enemy died in their hammocks.' Thus wrote Dr Campbell and the log of HMS *Dunkirk* provides melancholy evidence that he was right. During the week that she was on patrol near Mattalena, eleven men died: three on Monday, one on Tuesday, two on Wednesday, one on Friday 29, two on Saturday, two more on Sunday. Thus it continued for day after day as bodies were dropped into the sea and the survivors bid generously for 'Dead Men's Cloaths', knowing that the proceeds of the auction would provide some measure of support for the widows and orphans of their shipmates, when HMS *Dunkirk* eventually returned to port.

I sense a particular poignancy – a sad recklessness – in the fact that two cheerful gamblers rattled the dice on the quarterdeck while their friends were dying down below, and that two other officers stood by, engrossed in the game of backgammon. Did they calculate the probability of who would be next to die, or consult *The Doctrine of Chances* for an appropriate equation? Friday's victim, Charles Garnes, breathed his last at four o'clock in the morning, in the hour before dawn when so many others drifted into death, in the dark, cramped, fetid quarters which they shared with the massive guns; but the four friends gathered on the quarterdeck seem to have survived.

I cannot be sure, since the muster lists are imperfect and there is a certain amount of guesswork involved, but I think I may have identified at least some of this motley crew. The odds were stacked against me, since the only record that any of them had ever been on board HMS *Dunkirk*, even as supernumeraries, was the mention of William Stafford, a year earlier – and none were listed among the officers of the *York*, the *Suffolk* or the *Experiment*. I was particularly puzzled by Captain Bolling, since no one of that name was commissioned in the Royal Navy, at any time in the eighteenth century, and I began to wonder whether he might have been a military man.

But there was no sign of any Bolling amongst the officers of the British Army.

In desperation I typed 'Bolling' into the search engine of my computer, and found myself inundated with possibilities, all of whom came from West Virginia. That gave me the clue I needed. I remembered that a member of the Gooch family, from whose library the book had come, had been Lieutenant Governor of Virginia in the eighteenth century. I checked the auction catalogue for further details and discovered to my joy that Sir William Gooch, the Lieutenant Governor, was dispatched with a regiment of Virginian troops to Jamaica (where he arrived at the beginning of 1741), and that he was badly injured in the attack on Cartagena. Gooch's lamentations from the Caribbean, preserved in the National Archives, provide vivid testimony to the mismanagement of this ill-fated expedition.

'We found no orders lodged for a supply of either Money or Provisions [and] we have been able to raise but £2,000, for which we are very much obliged to Mr Manning a Merchant of Kingston.' Thus wrote Gooch to the Duke of Newcastle, on 7 January 1741, shortly after his arrival in Jamaica. He also recorded the first casualties of this unhealthy climate: 'We have buried in this Island nine officers and about one hundred men.' Five months later, in June, Gooch was back in Jamaica and keen to disassociate himself from the disasters of Cartagena, 'which I imagine will be differently reported by our two Chiefs'. He grumpily reminded the Duke that he himself had been excluded from the Council of War ('after commanding for so many years was obliged to obey') and spent the rest of the letter complaining about his leg injury.

'Finding my Constitution much Impaired by the Fatigue I underwent from a broiling sun upon a Sand, to which I had been exposed for many days together before the accident, and my confinement since; as I am fitter for an Hospital than anything else, I am going, with our Commanders Leave to my Government, to try if the winter, cold Baths, and a change of air, in the opinion of the Doctors the only Remedys, will be of any service to me; tho I apprehend from my present Condition, I shall never perfectly recover the use of my right Leg.'

Eureka! The proof of Gooch's presence at Cartagena, commanding a regiment from Virginia, provided the beginnings of an answer as to how my copy of *The Doctrine of Chances* had found its way from the deck of an eighteenth-century warship to a library in Suffolk; but it all depended on finding the right Captain Bolling. Here I had a bonus. Having sifted through dozens of different Bollings I discovered that the only feasible candidate added an almost mythical ancestry to the cumulative improbabilities of this complex story.

John Bolling was born in West Virginia in 1700 and married at the age of twenty-eight to Mary Elizabeth Blair. The first of their twenty children arrived a year later and was christened Matoaka, one of the names originally borne by her most famous forebear – for 'Capt. Bolling' proved to be none other than the great-great-grandson of the most fabled romance in England's colonial history, the marriage of John Rolfe and the Powhatan 'princess', Pocahontas.

Bolling followed a military career (eventually being promoted to Major) but seldom served far from home, judging by the babies; for his long-suffering wife was pregnant almost every year, thrice with twins. But there was an unusual gap between the birth of their eleventh child, in August 1738, and that of the twelfth, in September 1742. Captain Bolling was off to the wars with Colonel Gooch, and Mary Elizabeth was given a brief respite.

Contingents from Gooch's regiment were dispersed throughout Vernon's fleet. On 24 January 1741, at Port Royal Harbour in Jamaica, HMS *Dunkirk* had embarked 'Supernumerys, being Fifty-one Soldiers belonging to Coll Wm Gooch's Regiment' to join the smaller group of 'Marines, belonging to Coll Wm Robinson's Regiment' which had boarded the ship the previous October, in England. Similar numbers were allocated to the *Suffolk*, *York* and *Experiment*, but Captain Bolling's name is missing from these muster lists. How did he come to be aboard HMS *Dunkirk* on 29 May? I can only guess that in the aftermath of the attack on Cartagena, some of the sick and wounded from the original contingents of Gooch's men had been transferred to other ships, heading back to Jamaica, while replacements were supplied to protect the rear-guard in case of attack, and that these movements are not fully recorded in the surviving documents.

I am forced to speculate, because I am faced with the inescapable evidence of that faded inscription on the flyleaf of De Moivre's book. Close inspection reveals that it was written by three different hands, probably as the memento of a brief moment of camaraderie before they all dispersed to their different ships. *Mr Mollet and Mr Dobby at Backgammon 29 May 1740 under the awning on board His Majesties Ship Dunkirk* – that neat, legible note was written, I feel sure, by one of the pair it mentions. It was immediately followed by the bold signature of another member of the party, *Capt. Bolling*. Then a cramped hand takes over, as an older man adds his name; *& Mr Stafford first Lieutenant looking on*. Messrs. Mollet and Dobby remain unidentified, unless the latter is a nickname for Arthur Dobbins, who was the Purser of HMS *Suffolk*. Captain Bolling was a member of Gooch's regiment and First Lieutenant Stafford was probably an officer in the Marines.

Lurking somewhere at the margins of this game of back-gammon is the ghostly presence of a fifth person, the owner of the book. I briefly considered the *Dunkirk*'s Captain, Thomas Cooper, but the elegance of the book's original binding suggested that it belonged to a man of greater wealth. My guess is that Captain Bolling had borrowed *The Doctrine of Chances* from Colonel Gooch and that eventually, after all these adventures were over, he managed to return it to him, at the Governor's Mansion in Williamsburg. Gooch returned to England in 1747, a rich baronet, laden with possessions – fine furniture, portraits of himself, silver and gold plate, and his library. Sir William's surviving correspondence suggests a highly intelligent man but it is also clear that his sense of his own achievements was shaded by sadness; Virginia had made his fortune but claimed the life of his only son and heir. All his worldly goods were inherited by a nephew, in Suffolk.

As so often happens when an old man dies childless, stories were lost – but here as a postscript is one that I may have invented, to fill the gap. Towards the end of the seventeenth century William Gooch was living in London, about to embark on a military career. He had been decently educated at the grammar school in Great Yarmouth but it was felt that he needed further study in mathematics, and a friend of the family recommended a tutor. Thus it was that Gooch came to meet an eccentric émigré Frenchman, who walked between the houses of his pupils with the pages of Newton's *Principia* stuffed in his pockets, had a fascination for games of chance, and spent the whole of his long life trying 'to distinguish Truth from what seems so nearly to resemble it'.

There is a strange, personal addition to this sequence of chances. Some time after completing my research I was looking in a file of miscellaneous family papers when my eye was caught by a brief reference to my namesake and distant ancestor, Lieutenant-Colonel Simon Loftus of the 15th Foot. With a shudder almost of apprehension I read the details of his death – in Jamaica, in 1741, of wounds sustained at the siege of Cartagena – where he commanded a contingent of Irish troops that included his youngest son, Dudley; who was killed within sight of his father.

Reading Gardner's *History*

'The Study of *Antiquity* being generally agreeable to the Disposition of many ingenious People, I have presumed to publish this small Tract of some Places, especially the once famous CITY of DUNWICH, which will afford Speculation sufficient to ruminate on the Vicissitude, and Instability of sublunary Things.'

That wonderful sentence, reminiscent of the seventeenth-century Norfolk polymath Sir Thomas Browne, opens the Preface to Thomas Gardner's *Historical Account of Dunwich, Blithburgh, Southwold*, published in 1754. This masterpiece of local history quotes from numerous documents that have long since vanished and explores byways of social history that are recorded nowhere else. It prompts the 'Speculation' that Gardner loved.

I speculate, first of all, on Gardner himself. Who was this extraordinary man?

Born in 1690, he first appears in the records in 1729, when he was appointed Town Constable. The municipal offices followed in swift succession – Deputy Controller of the Port of Southwold, Sergeant at Arms, Fen Reeve, Member of the Assembly, Inspector of the Work-House and Salt Tax Officer. In 1756 he was elected Churchwarden and the following year was one of the Bailiffs of Southwold. Two years later he was appointed Chamberlain, responsible for keeping the town accounts. So this was a capable and highly respected man, trusted by his fellow townsmen, or at least by those who controlled the affairs of the Borough.

Gardner was also a down-to-earth person, with fingers in many pies, as was typical of the time. Described as a 'joiner' for much of his life, he supplied building materials for the Church, repaired the town windmill and seems to have acted in some respects as an undertaker. On several occasions there were payments to Gardner for making coffins and to his second wife Molly for making shifts – probably shrouds. Like most who could afford it, he also owned a share in a boat – the sloop 'John & Sarah'.

These glimpses suggest a practical man, perhaps the equivalent of a local builder, but there was another side to him, the scholar and historian. In 1745, he exhibited 'A true and exact plate, containing the boundaries of the town of Dunwich, and the entries of certain records and evidences' at the Society of Antiquaries in London. This was the first public evidence of what became his consuming passion – a history of his town and locality.

It must have been about this time that Gardner was appointed the Salt Tax Officer. It was a position of some importance when the tax on salt was a significant stream of government revenue, and it demanded rigorous integrity. Salt destined for the fishing fleet was exempt from the tax, so Gardner needed a watchful eye to ensure that John May, owner of the Southwold salt works, wasn't fiddling his books and selling tax-free salt for domestic use.

Gardner's role became increasingly important after 1750, when Southwold was chosen as the headquarters of the Free British Fishery, established by Act of Parliament. The object was to revive the nation's fishing industry and compete with the Dutch, our longstanding rivals for dominance of the European herring markets. £500,000 was voted for the endeavour, equivalent to almost £100 million in modern money.

Wharves and warehouses, a net house, tan office, cooper's workshop and a row of cottages in Church Street were built for this new venture, and the entrance to Southwold's harbour was improved by the completion of two piers. Fifty large busses (broad-beamed herring boats) were constructed and fitted out, and the Salt Works vastly increased its production. We can guess that the increased responsibilities of his role may have allowed Gardner to employ a clerk to undertake much of the work, leaving him time to pursue his passion as a historian, because the project that he had embarked on required an extraordinary amount of research – transcribing and summarising documents, examining buildings and ruins for traces of their past, collecting coins and curiosities and fossils, many of which he engraved as illustrations. It was a stupendous labour and Gardner was duly grateful to those who had made it possible. He published his masterpiece in 1754 and dedicated it to the Harbour Commissioners. It was financed by a long list of subscribers, headed by the 'His late Highness, Frederick Prince of Wales' – the first Governor of the Free British Fishery. Gardner's engraving of 'The Southwest Prospect of Southwold', which accompanied his history, showed all the new developments that the Fishery had brought to the town.

The book itself is elegantly printed (with occasionally erratic pagination) but it is clear that Gardner expected his readers to make notes in it, amplifying the text, because blank pages were bound in at frequent intervals, right from the start. In my own copy, those pages remain empty, as published, but in each of the four copies owned by Southwold Museum they have been annotated by later owners with additional information and two of these copies have been rebound, with numerous extra leaves inserted, together with engraved illustrations, printed handbills and other ephemera. The result is a fascinating resource for local historians.

Perhaps the most interesting of the Museum's copies is that which was formerly owned by Francis Henry Vertue (1822–94) and Dudley Collings (1870–1955), both of whom were Southwold surgeons and antiquaries. Vertue was also a Borough Magistrate, 'well known for his convictions regarding justice and right', and Dudley Collings was the founding Curator of the Museum.

Vertue extended Gardner's story into the nineteenth century, preserving ephemera that ranged from fierce polemics surrounding the reform of the Borough in 1835 to a newspaper cutting from March 1890, recording the death at ninety-three of the diarist James Maggs – and a bill for some bacon that

Maggs bought a few years before his death. Maggs's *Southwold Diaries* (subsequently published by the Suffolk Records Society) are among the Museum's greatest treasures, but his own copy of Gardner's *History* (with 'numerous manuscript additions and annotations' and 'additional printed and manuscript tracts bound in') escaped our grasp. It came up for auction twenty years ago and fetched four times the high estimate. I should love to know where it can now be found.

As you can see, Gardner's own habit of digressions has rubbed off on me as I write, but at the back of my mind, all the time, is the mystery of the man himself, a question that remains unanswered. We know that he lived in a house in Park Lane, we know that he worked in the Salt Tax office on South Green, and we know that he died at the age of seventy-nine, on 30 March 1769, and was buried in Southwold churchyard between his two wives, Rachel and Mary. *Betwixt honour and virtue here doth lie, The remains of old antiquity.* But that beautiful phrase which I quoted at the beginning – that his book 'will inform Speculation sufficient to ruminate on the Vicissitude, and Instability of sublunary things' – continues to haunt me. Who was this man – on the one hand so practical and competent, on the other so buried in dusty documents and history – yet capable of writing those words – words which seem to echo Thomas Browne and anticipate W. G. Sebald?

That sense of a thread through time is embodied in the tale of a strange discovery (an echo of Browne's *Urne-Buriall*) with which Gardner ends his account of Dunwich. 'Within the walls of the *Grey Friars* at *Dunwich*, a Labourer discovered a small earthen Vessel, which he thinking contained Treasure, broke into Shreds. On the Top of it was a flat Piece of Brass, with the dimension of and Inscription on this Figure.' The 'figure' is an engraving by Gardner of a medieval ring brooch, with an undecipherable inscription on one side and, on the other, the words *Ave Maria Gracia Plena* (Hail Mary full of Grace). And he adds an intriguing note, without explanation, that 'The heart of Dame *Hawise Poynings* was reposited at this Place.'

It reads like a mystery, a brief glimpse of an unrecoverable past, but in 2004 this same bronze brooch reappeared at auction, together with a copy of Gardner's *History*. It had been handed down from one Suffolk antiquary to another, lovingly cherished, until it was sold for £3,000.

Brief Lives

I love old graveyards, especially those that have not been tidied up. I like the humpy ground, the stoop and totter of disordered headstones, the decayed splendour of family tombs. I relish the vigour of stone-carved lettering, spelling out the evocative names and comforting, customary phrases – or bursting the bounds of decorum with startling frankness, or a brief, heartrending sigh. That vivid immediacy is found surprisingly often in the country churchyards of East Suffolk or inside the churches themselves, etched on memorial slabs sunk into cool floors. It's part of the long local tradition of religious and political nonconformity – plain speaking, but with an ear for the rhythms of language.

These inscriptions can be quietly poignant or fiercely down-to-earth, or surprising in other ways. You might not expect to find evidence of the Industrial Revolution in the graveyard of

Leiston church but a couple of cast iron headstones, with bold nineteenth-century lettering, tell their own fascinating story. They were made in Garrett's engineering works, a thriving local business that was soon to become famous for its traction engines, exported to half the world. One of these gravestones commemorates a young man called Robert Fletcher (lovely medieval surname, meaning arrow-maker) and the other is a memorial to Henry Newson, who died in 1834 after a long but troubled life; 'No more we hear his spirit moan, His doubts and fear forever gone'. Nearby stands a rectangular stone pedestal, crowned with an elegant iron urn. The pedestal is inscribed with the names of various members of the Garrett family and the urn was cast in their factory – which was founded in 1778 when Richard Garrett married Elizabeth Newson and set up in business as a blacksmith and maker of agricultural tools.

A grandson of that marriage was the great Newson Garrett, who was born in Leiston in 1812 but found the village too crowded with his relatives, so moved to nearby Aldeburgh and made his fortune as a merchant and maltster. He was remembered by all who knew him as a good and generous man and is commemorated in Aldeburgh church with a lovely epitaph – 'God gave him largeness of heart'. Outside, in the graveyard, he lies buried alongside his wife and two of his children, one of whom was the remarkable Elizabeth Garrett Anderson. She became the first English woman to qualify as a doctor (in the face of strong opposition from the medical profession) and founded the first hospital in London to be staffed entirely by women – before retiring to Aldeburgh where she completed her pioneering career as the first woman mayor of any English town.

Her father's finest memorial is not in fact in Aldeburgh, for Newson Garrett was the man who built Snape Maltings, one of the grandest of its day, to supply the raw material for brewers in East Anglia and London. Here and there, if you look closely, you will find iron wall-ties embossed with his name, dotting the brick walls of foyers and performance spaces that have been converted from the kiln rooms and drying floors of the old Maltings. Garrett's 'largeness of heart' is everywhere implicit in the beauty of these fine industrial buildings – and wonderfully expressed in the series of portraits that he commissioned of his workers, which now hang in the foyer of the Maltings Concert Hall.

That sense of honour for manual work has a strong Suffolk tradition. Few visitors to the Concert Hall bother to stop at Snape Church, but here you can find a beautiful monument of rustic simplicity – a crumbly red headstone which marks the grave of George Alabaster, who died at the age of thirty-seven in 1759. It is carved with the tools of his trade, a pick and shovel.

Such unpretentious expressions of local worth take many forms. One of my favourite examples is the tomb of a seventeenth-century rector who was turned out of his living because of his loyalty to King Charles I, during the English Civil War. It is built into the south facing wall of Theberton church, close to the porch, and made like a bench, where visitors can pause and enjoy the warmth of the sun. 'Here is a stone to sitt upon, Under which lies in hopes to rise, To ye day of Blisse and Happinesse, Honest John Fenn.'

Continue up the road to Blythburgh church and you will find, close to the altar, the memorial stone of Thomas Neale of Bramfield, 'one of the Best of Magistrates in his time ...

who lived much desired and died greatly lamented'. Who could wish for a finer epitaph? But Neale suffered sadness, for close by lies his daughter Mary, 'who with a Straine of piety far beyond her years & a chearfulness to Admiration humbly Resigned her Soule into the hands of her Redeemer' – in June 1694 – 'Aged tenn years 4 months & 22 days'. The counting of every day of that short life tells us more than any words how she was loved and mourned.

A few miles away, in Neale's home village of Bramfield, is a hidden treasure – the most startling collection of epitaphs in the whole of Suffolk. To discover them you must make your way past all the other glories of this tiny church (detached round tower, one of the loveliest rood screens in England and magnificent sculptured monuments to Arthur Coke and his beloved wife, who died in childbirth) and concentrate your attention on the floor, immediately in front of the altar. Here, side by side, were buried the members of one of Bramfield's most prominent families – distant cousins of the great Nelson. And here, on the black slate slabs that cover their graves, we can read their lives, summarised with an urgency and eloquence that rings through the centuries. Linking those stories is a scandal, which someone wished remembered.

Whoever that 'someone' was seems to have had extraordinary licence to write the frankest epitaphs, mostly with affection but once with barely concealed disdain, and you must read them all to understand the hidden narrative, which links them. I like to begin with the memorial to Lambert Nelson who died in his fifties, in 1714. Lambert was a lawyer who married a local heiress, daughter of the delightfully named Reginald Rabett, and together they produced four children.

Thus far the inscription is entirely conventional, but then the author launches into a eulogy for a good but unrecognised man. It is worth quoting in full.

> He was a Man of bright Parts, sound judgement, Good Breeding and Pleasant Conversation, Master of the Learned Languages & all ye Liberal Arts, Yet a very Valuable and Right Honest Attorney.

I love that telling 'yet', as if it were astonishing that a man so gifted could also be that rarest of things, an honest lawyer.

> He was Second to None in the strokes of the pen Or Turns of Witt. A true Son of the Church and a Conscientous Subject Of the Crown of England: In either of which Capacities, He was fit for any Emploiment, Had he been less Reserv'd himself, Or better known in time to any Great Minister, Whose Height might expose him To the Necessity of Leaning Sometimes Upon so Steady a Propp, And the Bosom of so Resolute a Confident.

Lambert had a sister, Bridgett, who never married but 'freely underwent the Care of a Wife and a Mother, and often the Fatigue of a True Friend, for any of her Acquaintance in Sickness or Distress.'

> She was a Devout Member of the Established Church, Charitable, Prudent, Chast, Active and remarkably Temperate; yet often Afflicted with great Sicknesses, And for above three Years before her Death, with a Dropsy, of which she Died after having been tapped five times.

This admirable but afflicted woman gave her name to her niece, Lambert's eldest daughter, whose memorial slab lies close to her aunt and is inscribed with this astonishing story.

Between the Remains of her Brother Edward, And of her Husband Arthur, Here lies the Body of Bridgett Applewhait, Once Bridgett Nelson.

After the Fatigues of a Married Life, Born by her with Incredible Patience, For four Years and three Quarters, bating three Weeks; And after the Enjoiment of the Glorious Freedom Of an Easy and Unblemisht Widowhood, For four Years and Upwards, She Resolved to run the Risk of a Second Marriage-Bed But Death forbad the Banns – And having with an Apoplectick Dart (The same Instrument, with which he had formerly Dispatch't her Mother) Touch't the most Vital part of Brain; She must have fallen Directly to the Ground (as one Thunder-strook) If she had not been Catch't and Supported by her Intended Husband. Of which Invisible Bruise, After a struggle for above Sixty Hours, With that Grand Enemy to Life (But the certain and Merciful Friend to Helpless Old Age) In Terrible Convulsions, Plaintive Groans or Stupefying Sleep, Without recovery of her Speech or senses, She Dyed on the 12th day of Sept in ye Year of Our Lord 1737 and of her own Age 44.

That justly celebrated inscription is so full of drama that it's easy to overlook the memorial to Bridgett's husband, Arthur Applewhaite, who lies beside her – but only by reading his inscription can you understand her own. For her 'Fatigues of a Married Life' were provoked by this mean man, who caused her much grief. Arthur's father was 'Favourite and Bailiff' of successive owners of the great estate of Heveningham Hall but Arthur himself, as a second son, had little hope of inheritance. His marriage to Bridgett Nelson was made with a sharp eye to her wealth, as 'sole heiress' to her father's estates. But they had no children, so Arthur's intention that his wife's lands would eventually revert to Applewhaite ownership was frustrated. Such was his rage that Arthur's last act was to collude with his father and brother in a legal action to leave his wife penniless. '(Having by his Father's Instigation made no will) He left no legacy But a Chancery-Suit with his Eldest Brother For her own Paternal Estates in this Town and Blyford.'

That scandalous land-grab seems to have failed, leaving Bridgett to enjoy her 'easy and unblemisht widowhood', but its memory lingered long and the unknown memorialist who composed these inscriptions seized the chance to record the truth. The story is there to be read, by all who care to do so.

Reader, What Art Thou?

It was the binding that hooked me – scarlet leather, lavishly decorated in gold, complete with its original metal clasp and with the date, 1786, stamped on the spine. Even better, this lovely pocketbook was described by the auctioneer as containing numerous blank pages. I bought it unseen, intending to fill it with my favourite inscriptions from Suffolk tombstones.

I discovered, when it arrived, that this gaudy eighteenth-century cover had been repurposed – its original contents removed and replaced with a nineteenth-century notebook. And I found, to my delight, that some of those 'blank' pages were filled with intriguing transcripts of Norfolk epitaphs, recorded in the summer of 1832. Someone else had preceded my intention.

I decided to investigate its history.

To begin with I considered the binding and learnt that this highly distinctive style was sometimes used for pocket Almanacs, published annually by the Worshipful Company of Stationers in London, towards the end of the eighteenth century. Almanacs rapidly become dated, so a frugal nineteenth-century Norfolk man had simply extracted the obsolete contents and sewn in place a blank notebook of identical dimensions, to take with him on his explorations of the local graveyards. I thought about the ghost book, the missing almanac, and the events of 1786 – the premiere of Mozart's *Marriage of Figaro*, the death of Frederick the Great, the formal establishment of a penal colony in Botany Bay and the publication of Rabbie Burns' *Address to a Haggis*. None of these were predicted in any of the dozen almanacs published for that year by the Company of Stationers. These ranged from the useful ('the proper Days and Hours for transfering Stocks and receiving Dividends') to the arcane – 'Astrological Observations on the Four Quarters of the Year; an HIEROGLYPHIC alluding to the Present Times; and other Matters both Curious and profitable.' There was even an almanac for 'Ladies' – 'Containing new improvements in arts and sciences, and many entertaining particulars: designed for the use and diversion of the fair sex.' Any one of these intriguing publications might originally have been housed in my binding, but the possibility that it had once embellished a copy of the *Woman's Almanack* caused me to wonder whether the epitaphs, inscribed in faded ink on the pages of the inserted notebook, were written by a 'Lady'.

The first record, for a grave at New Buckenham, described *A tombstone with a figure very rudely done, scratching his Head or pulling off his Hair* – an image of the grief-stricken father of *Edwd Henry Dodd 1802 aged 14 yrs*. And so it continued, record after record of lives cut short, dismal proof of the high level of child mortality; including the three unnamed children of John & Mary Hardingham, suddenly dead.

> We took the Cup of life to sip
> Too bitter 'twas to drain,
> We put it meekly from our lips,
> And went to sleep again.

That sense of escaping a world of pain was a frequent theme, for young and old alike – none more so than in these brief, bleak lines

> In memory of Samuel Jouling
> Who left this world crying & howling.

But death was faced and confronted, again and again, in words that echoed the defiant cry engraved on Rachel Wilson's stone at Long Sutton, in 1826. It reads like a brilliant précis of John Donne's famous sonnet, *Death be not Proud*.

> Boast not, O Death, thy universal reign
> Thou in thy turn must fall – we rise again.

And then, in a wonderful change of mood, I came across this description of a tomb at Aylsham, memorial to a man who loved the world.

In a small garden enclosed in Iron railings close to the church (in beauty blooming 8th July 1832) are deposited the mortal remains of Humphry Repton Esq of Hare Street in the County of Essex – who died the 24th March 1818 aged 67 yrs –

> Not like the Egyptian Tyrants consecrate
> Unmixed with others shall my dust remain
> But moulding, blending, melting into Earth
> Mine shall give form and colour to the rose
> And while its vivid blossoms cheer mankind
> Its perfumed odours shall ascend to Heaven

Those are Repton's own words, inscribed above his last and smallest garden; rejoicing that his corpse would be compost – 'moulding, blending, melting into earth' – to fertilise the roses which still, miraculously, survive. 'In beauty blooming'. It is the legacy of a man whose famous 'red books', with their 'before' and 'after' views of his clients' estates, convinced them to transform the English landscape according to his own visions of an earthly paradise. I am reminded that my mother, another gardener, wanted her tombstone to be engraved with the words 'Feed the humble worm'. We translated the phrase into Latin to avoid arguments with the church authorities.

The description of Repton's memorial lingered happily in my mind as I thumbed my way through numerous blank pages to the end of the notebook and there discovered a surprise. On the very last page, as if deliberately hidden from view, I read these words.

Age of Cork Leg
new – Nov 1854
Wooden peg Leg
Feby 20th 1860

Our antiquarian friend, who I now felt sure was a man, must have lost a leg about twenty years after his visits to those Norfolk graveyards and was forced to make do with a prosthetic. He began with an expensive 'Cork Leg', so-called, 'not because they were made of cork, for they were not, but because the best kind of them were made in London in Cork Street'. I am quoting Dickens, from *Little Dorrit*.

Cork Street now is filled with smart galleries but in the early nineteenth century nine fashionable tailors had set up shop there – so perhaps it seemed natural to have a leg made to fit at the same time as ordering a new coat. The elegantly shaped and polished legs for which the street was famous had metal joints, allowing a degree of articulation, but for that very reason were prone to disintegrate over time. Hence the fact that after six years' use the owner of this notebook settled for a sturdy peg leg – the sort that served Long John Silver.

He recorded the purchase of his legs in the same elegant hand as the earlier graveyard inscriptions. There is a lightness of touch – a feeling of pleasure in use of the pen – with none of the crabbed constriction indicative of age and ill temper. I began to feel I knew the man and should have liked him.

Part of that liking was because reading his notes, jotted down nearly two hundred years ago, I had been imagining someone who shared my own relish for the idioms of the past – but suddenly I realised that for him the past was recent.

Humphry Repton died a mere fourteen years before his epitaph was recorded in this notebook; the writer was no antiquarian.

So who was he, or she, and what was the motive for these jottings? I have a sense of cheerful curiosity, a fascination for the oddities of their own time, delight in the forthright language of these memorials. Nothing mealy-mouthed.

Whoever wrote or carved those words knew that they would be read by neighbours who had lived alongside the dead, known them well, and could not be gulled with fancy phrases. So when Eliz[abeth] Gunton died in 1810, aged sixty-nine, her relatives made no attempt to extol a very private or perhaps very difficult woman. Instead, they set us a challenge.

What kind of person she was the day of Judgement
will discover.
Reader, what art thou?

Travels

Sunday Afternoon

On a sleepy Sunday in Marseille, as the sun slanted through a gap in the shutters, the golden-haired girl beside me rose from the bed to get dressed. 'Where are you from?' she asked. 'Angleterre,' I murmured. 'O you poor thing,' she cried as she crossed herself. 'How terrible to live in a country where no one believes in God.'

1974

Guess the Century

Half a dozen people sit enthralled at the dinner table while Madame Dubois Challon talks about chickens. She complains that Pascal Delbeck, the young manager of her estates, has insisted that her little farm in the Entre Deux Mers is capable of producing more than a few eggs for her table, that he wants to make serious wine there. So the chickens must go. Her hands gesture rapidly as they try to keep up with her tongue and its expressive volubility. She calls us 'mes enfants' and looks brightly round the table, happy to see her guests enjoying themselves, before launching into another entertaining story or item of local gossip. Pascal, meanwhile, smiles enigmatically within his glossy black beard and goes to the kitchen to fetch another decanter of wine.

This one is poured with a little more care than the others and we are all attentive. Even Madame, who treats the

treasured wines that she offers us with the blithest insou-
ciance, pauses long enough to sniff, to sip, and to exclaim
'Sensationnel,' before resuming her interrupted conversation
with Madame Meneret. 'Moi, j'adore les betteraves [beetroot].'

The rest of us are trying to guess the vintage. The colour
has the red-brown tint of full maturity and this impression of
elegant age is confirmed by nose and palate. But the wine has
tremendous individuality and is still full of life, with a sweet
aroma of strawberries and dried rose petals. It grows in the
glass, eclipsing even the very grand wines that have preceded it.

'Pre-war,' says someone, but which war? We start guessing.
'1934,' ventures one of the guests, '29' says another. Knowing
this château's reputation for longevity I suggest one of those
fabled years, 1899 or 1900. '1870,' is my desperate final bid,
remembering an extraordinary Latour of that vintage, still
vivid after a century. A small shake of the head, a smile. '49,'
he announces quietly. '1849.'

Only here, at Ausone, could such an astounding wine be
offered so casually and, for a brief time, before it faded, be
enjoyed with such enthusiasm. Even were it possible to find
a bottle of comparable age in the cellars of another château,
the likelihood that it would be drinkable (137 years old, from
a year that Michael Broadbent described as 'a moderate, ordi-
nary vintage') would be remote in the extreme. But Ausone
is a special case and this ancient wine is not only alive, but
enchanting.

The cellars from which it came are huge, cavernous vaults
excavated in the sixteenth century from the limestone rock of
a steep hill above the town of St Emilion. In this dark, cool
and humid place, wine matures exceptionally slowly, in cask

and bottle, and gradually achieves the sort of complexity for which great claret is renowned.

The story is full of improbable elements. For over a hundred years Ausone has been ranked as one of the great wines of Bordeaux, on a par with Cheval Blanc as the best of St Emilion. But in the 1960s and '70s it was inconsistent to the point of mediocrity. There were good reasons. Before the boom of the seventies, times were hard, particularly for the smaller estates, aggravated by some truly dreadful vintages. In 1963, 1965 and 1968 no wine was judged good enough to sell under the Ausone label – the harvest of those years was disposed of in bulk, to the négociants, for less than the cost of production. Even in the good years it was hard to make a profit, so it was impossible to find the resources to invest in replanting, re-equipment and the replacement of casks.

There were other problems, particular to the place. Though the early seventies brought better prices the owner, Monsieur Dubois Challon, was by then a sick man. Until his death in 1974 he required a great deal of care, leaving his wife neither time nor energy to turn her mind to improving the management of the estate. The regisseur was in his eighties and the cellar-master was unsuited to his task. When I visited Ausone at that time he seemed more interested in cultivating his mushrooms than looking after the wine.

Soon after her husband's death, however, Madame Dubois Challon took matters in hand and made an appointment of startling audacity. In 1975 she engaged a nineteen-year-old viticultural student, Pascal Delbeck, as assistant to her aged manager and in the following year gave him complete charge. She backed him in his appointment of one of the youngest teams of any of the great Bordeaux châteaux and in various improvements that he wished to make. Her choice was a resounding success. The 1976 Ausone was hailed as one of the best wines of its vintage, and in subsequent years the quality has been maintained at the highest level, though sometimes overlooked by the critics, because Pascal prefers elegance to force of expression, and his wines can take many years to reveal their full potential.

The production is tiny and you need a great deal of patience, for after the first explosive delight of the new wine, Ausone becomes closed, unyielding, impenetrable. Decades later, when mature, you are presented with one of the most individual of the great Bordeaux – combining a gamey mélange of autumnal scents and flavours, cedar wood and tobacco, with the sweet aromas of dried fruit and flowers.

The dramatic change of fortunes in Ausone's reputation has had no apparent effect on the unpretentious appeal of the place itself. When I went to thank Madame Dubois Challon, the morning after that memorable dinner, she opened the door of an old cupboard to show me some precious porcelain, stacked alongside a ball of twine and her gardening gloves. Then she emerged, elegantly dressed, chattering like a bird, and drove off to have lunch with friends in Bordeaux – while Pascal, having won his point about chickens, planned a modest revolution in Entre Deux Mers.

When we left the previous evening, he presented me with the beautiful hand-blown bottle in which the 1849 Ausone had lain for over a century. At midnight, long after the wine was gone, it still smelt faintly of roses.

Pale olive in colour, with a tall 'punt' at the base, it sits on my desk as I write. For the first time I notice, amidst a swirl of imperfections, a large air bubble trapped in the thickness of the glass. One careless knock, any time in the past 130 years, and we should all have been denied the most extraordinary taste of our lives.

1986

In the Heart of Gascony

The Gers is a land of rolling hills, wide skies and clear air. In the far distance, defining the horizon, the Pyrenees; bright and glistening with snow, or dark and looming, or floating like a mirage above clouds and mist, or invisible, shrouded in a blue haze. Threading through these hills, spreading like a fan from the mountains, are dozens of rivers and streams. The mightiest of these, the Garonne, curves around the region's eastern flank, through Toulouse, and then turns west, towards distant Bordeaux. The most beautiful, the Adour, runs north from Tarbes along the western borders of the Gers, sparkling over its bed of rounded stones, shaded by poplars and willows. Kingfishers dart across the river in a flash of green; white egrets stand motionless until disturbed, when they heave themselves into the air, croaking like old men. And sometimes, high above, you can see the cranes on their annual migration, calling constantly.

Water is ever present, greening this southern land, but it is the shape of the hills that lingers in the mind – undulating, rippling, rolling in endless variety. These are not daunting peaks, closing off the sky, but the waves of an open landscape, limestone under clay, catching the light and dappled by the shadows of the passing clouds. The hills are a patchwork of meadows and cornfields and vineyards, patterned by hedgerows and crowned with stands of trees. Oaks are everywhere – black oak, evergreen oak – but so too are horse chestnuts and walnuts, poplars and plane trees, tall cypress and prickly holly. Hiding in the woods are badgers, deer, wild boar and a great many owls.

The climate is seldom grey but can be extreme. In summer the clay dries and cracks in the heat of the sun, bakes hard as iron, but in spring and winter the rains can turn it to sticky glue, which clings lovingly to your boots – they call it the 'terre amoureuse'. But the rain ceases as swiftly as it came and then the air is clear again, and sparkling.

The Gers is a place of passage, at the midpoint between the Atlantic and the Mediterranean, near the mountain passes between France and Spain. Huge flocks of palombes (migrant wood pigeons) fly north from the Pyrenees as the swallows head south, and others have traversed these hills for all manner of reasons, fleeing from persecution or in search of salvation, like those who still follow the pilgrims' paths to Santiago de Compostela, the routes of St James. Some of these migrants remain – you can recognise names that are Italian or Spanish or Breton in origin – but there has also been an exodus, and this is one of the few places in Europe that has a smaller population now than it did a hundred years ago. Gascons have always been tough, and many left to make a living elsewhere when times were hard. That tradition is romanticised in tales of d'Artagnan and the 'Cadets de Gascogne', but there is another tradition, equally strong, which is the openness and welcome of those who have stayed, to newcomers and strangers. This, to me, is one of the most alluring aspects of the Gers – the frankness and generosity of its people, the lack of suspicion, a willingness to take time. They joke about this unhurried way of doing things; an appointment to meet 'in a quarter of an hour' carries no promise of promptness. When the siren sounds at midday from the roof of every Mairie, it is the start of the two-hour lunch.

And what a lunch it can be. This is the land of ceps and asparagus, cassoulet and duck confit, fat geese and round cheeses, sweet croustade, good wine and heart-warming Armagnac. A healthy appetite and a restful view of the world provide a generous rebuke to the press and hurry of the city.

In fact there are no cities in the Gers. The region's capital, Auch, is little more than a large town and the rest are villages, even when, as in Eauze, the church is so large that they call it a cathedral. And you arrive at the villages as you did in medieval times, quite suddenly – one minute you are in the country, the next you are in the market place. There is none of that depressing sprawl of industrial estates and superstores.

Several of these villages have a surprisingly formal plan (a grid of streets around a single, central square) quite unlike the tangle of twisting alleys of older, more haphazard settlements. These walled bastides were founded in the late thirteenth and early fourteenth centuries as plantation towns in frontier territory – colonising and fortifying the western borders of Gascony against incursions from Aquitaine, which was ruled by the English. New settlers were promised freedom from local taxes and given a plot of land to build on, an adjacent plot for a garden, and a few hectares to cultivate, outside the town.

Marciac, now famous for jazz, is a classic bastide. As you explore its streets, peering over walls, you can recognise the original settler's pattern of house and garden, replicated in unexpected ways. You might spot a few rows of cabbages and artichokes, or half a dozen chickens, scratching the soil – the countryside contained within the town. One evening on my way to supper I glanced through a gate in a side street and discovered a farmyard, where Monsieur Dupouy keeps his cows. It was past dusk and a light was burning at the far end of the yard, silhouetting the old man – small, bent and wearing his Gascon beret. He caught sight of me and beckoned me in.

'Ah M'sieur, it's a lot of work. I am often here until nine thirty at night.' He spoke in a rush of words, thick with the southern twang.

Monsieur Dupouy takes his cattle to pasture every day, as his predecessors have done for centuries past, and brings them back at night, to sleep in the town. Five cows were crammed into the old byre. Four were the cream-coloured breed that you see in all the local fields but the fifth was blue-brown and gleaming, a huge horned beast with the archaic beauty of a Sumerian carving. For a moment time seemed to flicker, as I gazed at the past.

The heart of Marciac is its arcaded square. The old market building that used to shade the produce stalls was demolished in the early years of the twentieth century (an act of municipal vandalism) but the market itself still takes place on Wednesdays, as decreed when the town was founded, seven hundred years ago. Some of the vendors sell cheap clothes made in China but the travelling butcher and fishmonger will also be there and you can still find local cheeses, including a delicious brebis from the Pyrenees, or a trestle table covered in strawberries, or a stall with a pile of ceps. And if you are hungry you can enjoy a pizza, cooked on the spot in a wood-fired oven, which blazes away in the corner of a drop-sided van, in defiance of a catalogue of regulations that no one wants to know about. Or you can relax over a glass of wine or a hot chocolate, under the arcades, and watch the world go by.

Around the square, under these arcades, you may find various shops including an excellent baker (try their tourte maison), a couple of cafés and a restaurant – which at the time of writing had the startling distinction of an English girl in charge of the kitchen, something that would have been inconceivable in rural France even a few years ago. And of course there is the Mairie, centre of Marciac's administration and base for its dynamic mayor, Jean-Louis Guilhaumon.

It was Guilhaumon who somehow decided that a village of 1200 inhabitants was the obvious place to host one of the world's most renowned Jazz Festivals. He started the first festival in 1978 and has seen it grow to the point that the place goes completely crazy for the first two weeks of August. Every day for a fortnight the market square hosts free concerts from morning till evening, and every square inch of the pavements is filled with tables and chairs, as thousands of visitors eat and drink in the welcome shade of its ancient arcades. And then, as dusk draws near, everyone moves to a huge marquee (le chapiteau) on the nearby rugby pitch, where up to 5000 fans cram in to listen to some of the greatest names in jazz, and many more picnic outside, in the summer night. Previous 'greats' have included Lionel Hampton, Dizzy Gillespie, Stan Getz, Oscar Peterson, Stéphane Grappelli, Keith Jarrett, Wynton Marsalis, Ray Charles, Nina Simone, Ibrahim Ferrer.

What makes it special is that the whole town takes part. Houses are thrown open for impromptu bed-and-breakfast accommodation, or are turned into cafés, and groups of jazz musicians suddenly strike up in the most unexpected places. Everyone is made welcome. And afterwards, when the visitors have gone, the local children learn to play jazz in school, as part of their normal curriculum. It is the most astonishing achievement.

Gascony takes delight in digressions – so the road from Marciac to Auch can be a relatively straightforward route, taking less than an hour, but the best way to enjoy it is to allow yourself to be sidetracked.

The first stage takes you to the village of Bassoues, an enchanting road that meanders through lovely countryside and the tiny hamlet of Mascaras, a name that reminds me of black-streaked tears. Bassoues has the ancient covered market-place that Marciac, sadly, now lacks – and in this sense is a model of the classic bastide – but unlike most of the others it is dominated by a forbidding fortress tower, dating from the fourteenth century. Ignore the threatening past and climb to the top, to enjoy a magnificent view, for miles around.

This is the point at which you should take a deviation, retracing your steps for less than a couple of kilometres and then branching right, towards Lupiac. I love this road for its wide vistas and for the fine Romanesque church that you pass at the village of Peyrusse-Grande, and the sense of peace and timelessness. When you arrive in the tiny square of Lupiac you must doff your cap to a legend and drink a glass of Armagnac, for this was the birthplace of d'Artagnan. Find your way back to Bassoues by an alternative route and don't worry when you get lost, because it's such delightful country-side that it doesn't matter.

Through Montesquiou and Barran (another old covered-market, and a fortified gate) you arrive at Auch, capital of the Gers. This is a fine, dignified place and the road brings you straight to the centre, where a playful fountain constantly changes shape, in front of the cathedral. You could explore the twisting medieval streets of the old town, or relish the lively market if you happen to arrive on a Saturday, or admire the elaborate carving of the choir stalls in the cathedral, but it is probably time for lunch and these things can wait. So head for the Café Daroles, near the fountain.

This wonderful establishment has been in business since the end of the eighteenth century and it remains the epitome of the provincial café/restaurant. On a normal weekday at lunchtime the entire ground floor and first floor will be packed – and in summer you can eat on the pavement. Businessmen, couples, friends meet here as a matter of course, often several times a week, to enjoy the reassuring pleasures of a menu that hardly ever changes, the brisk and witty service of waiters and waitresses who dash up and down the stairs carrying plates and trays and bottles with careless proficiency, the brass-railed shelf behind the seats for hats and shopping, the faded photographs on the walls and the cunningly placed mirror to observe your fellow diners. These are the features of the classic brasserie, now increasingly rare and the more to be treasured. It feels like the France I once knew, forty years ago.

Autumn is the most wonderful season in the Gers – they call it the 'Gascon summer' – when the slanting light of the sun defines every fold and ripple of the land in sharp relief. It is the time of harvest, the vintage, the gathering of fruit and nuts, and hunting for fungi. And it is also the time when the hunters make elaborate preparations for the arrival of the palombes.

As I walked one of the numerous paths that thread this beautiful land I was dazzled by the brilliance of the horse-chestnut trees, their leaves turning gold, and by the shining conkers that littered the verges, wrapped in their spiky coverings. I crushed walnuts underfoot, and acorns, then turned up the side of a field, which was filled with the shrivelled stalks of maize, rustling like dead leaves. There was a patch of woodland on my right and a dry ditch, half hidden by the hedgerow.

Slowly I realised that along the entire length of this ditch was an elaborate hide, disguised by bracken. I found an opening and peered inside. There was a dining table, a rudimentary kitchen and somewhere to rest – all hidden in a long shady tunnel that ran up the side of the wood to the top of the hill. Just inside the entrance I spotted a crank handle, linked to a conveyor belt with paddles attached to it, which disappeared upwards, hidden in a pair of wide tubes. Then I noticed that what I had taken for thin tree trunks were in fact these plastic pipes, camouflaged with bark, rising to a perch in the branches of a nearby tree, also hidden from view. This was where the lookout would sit, watching for the pigeons, while his friends, the other hunters, made merry below. And this elaborate conveyor system was to keep him supplied with bottles of wine or Armagnac, sausages and bread, as he waited for the palombes.

I like to think that all that food and drink made the hunters miss their aim, and the pigeons flew by unharmed – but I, too, was a hunter, for a very different prey. Lurking amidst fallen leaves near the roots of oak trees, I was hoping to spot the gleaming buns of the region's noblest fungi, beautiful brown ceps.

But foraging can be tricky, for local farmers claim these treasures as their private property and are known to challenge those who pick them without permission. You may have to buy them from a stall in the market. Look for ceps that are dry, firm to touch and fresh to smell. They should not be at all sweaty and underneath their shining brown or cream-coloured caps they should still be pinkish grey, perhaps a hint of green – but before the green turns lurid, which it will begin to do within a day or two of being picked. Ceps that are slightly too old may be perfectly edible, delicious by most standards, but freshest are best.

Ceps should be prepared and cooked in front of your friends, as my Gascon friend Jeremy Hart did for us one night, when we had supper at his kitchen table. Clean off any dirt with a damp cloth or a small brush, but do not wash them. Trim off the very ends of the fat stalks and separate the stalks from the caps. Slice the stalks lengthways and the caps crossways with a sharp knife, quite thin. Chop up some garlic (which is grown in abundance in Gascony) and cook it in a thick-bottomed pan with a little olive oil. When the garlic is beginning to brown add the ceps to the pan (stalks and caps together), and turn them constantly until they begin to soften, then let them toast for a moment on fairly high heat. Don't cook them too long – the art is not to let them get soggy, but equally they should not be too dry. Stir in a handful of roughly chopped flat-leaf parsley and serve immediately, with good red wine.

It's a Gascon feast, one of the finest pleasures of the Gers.

2006

The Mysteries of Rayas

I tried to telephone (number unobtainable) and wrote to request a visit – no reply. So I took a chance and announced my intended arrival at 3 p.m. on a certain date in May, 1979. Despite losing my way and stopping several times to ask directions, I made it on time. The modest, ramshackle building was firmly shuttered and there was no sign of life, except the rasping of cicadas. I waited a while, without much hope, then turned the car to leave. As I did so, a very old man rose from a ditch beside the dusty track. The day was hot, but he was dressed in crumpled elegance – grey flannel trousers, old-fashioned striped shirt with collar and tie, linen jacket and a venerable Panama hat. He had the dignified but slightly bemused air of a time traveller from another age, an elderly lepidopterist who had mislaid his butterfly net.

'Monsieur Reynaud?', I hesitated. 'Oui, monsieur.' I asked

if it was possible to visit the chais and taste his wine. 'Non.' Without explanation but with great courtesy of manner he refused. I drove slowly down the lane and stopped at the corner to turn and wave. He had disappeared.

I treasure that memory because Louis Reynaud was one of the great traditionalists of Châteauneuf-du-Pape, and by far the most elusive. The fact that he had been there at the appointed time, waiting to refuse me entry, was a very rare honour, from a man notorious for shunning visitors.

He was equally averse to the authorities who laid down rules for wine production. His white wines included Chardonnay (not one of the thirteen permitted grape varieties of Châteauneuf-du-Pape) and the labels of Château Rayas proclaimed, quite illegally, that it was a 'Premier Grand Cru'. The magic words 'appellation contrôlée' were missing. To which Reynaud's response was uncompromising – 'Appellation contrôlée! C'est la guarantie du mediocrité!' But his wines were superb.

Louis Reynaud died soon after that brief encounter, and the estate was taken over by his son Jacques. I managed to obtain an occasional, modest allocation of some fabulous vintages, stretching back to 1957, but it took fifteen years before I was able to arrange a visit.

I arrived full of hope, in September 1994, thinking that I might finally be able to unravel the mysteries of Rayas. Almost immediately I realised that I was doomed to disappointment.

Jacques Reynaud was an enigma. Looking like a tramp but with the shy, confiding smile of a child, he made some of the most extraordinary wines of Châteauneuf apparently by chance, in ill-kempt cellars piled with rubbish. My tasting with him was a bizarrely random experience, with some wines superb, others out of condition. He poured a glass of Pignan, the second wine of Rayas, and I asked the vintage. Reynaud shrugged. 'Quatre-vingt onze, quatre-vingt douze, ça depend.' Depends on what, I wondered. Ambiguity clouded every utterance.

Not least of my perplexities was trying to understand the identities of his various wines.

A few facts were well established. I knew that the vineyards of Rayas itself (there is no Château) were situated in low hills to the north of the town of Châteauneuf; that the vines were grown on sandy, north-facing slopes, surrounded by pine trees; and that the famous galets roulés of Châteauneuf (large glacier-worn stones that elsewhere cover the vineyards, absorbing the heat of the day and radiating it back at night) were entirely absent from this cool, infertile terrain. All of which meant that the grapes took longer to ripen, building flavours of unusual purity and elegance.

I also knew that Reynaud owned a Côtes du Rhône estate, Fonsalette, but I learnt that there was another vineyard at Courthezon, not far from Château de Beaucastel but outside the Châteauneuf appellation. And then there was Pignan, ostensibly the second wine of Rayas, which sometimes tasted better than Rayas itself. There seemed no consistent logic to the labelling. I had to piece together the explanations, interpreting the secretive clues provided by Monsieur Reynaud, as we tasted from chipped glasses, briefly rinsed to remove some of the grime.

The red wine of Rayas was famous for being 100 per cent Grenache, from very old vines giving incredibly low yields. But I discovered that there was also a little Syrah, and a little Cinsault, the proportions of which might vary from year to year. I tasted the '93 Cinsault, unblended. It seemed the best wine of that vintage; juicy, elegant and alive. All three grapes were also planted at Fonsalette and normally combined together, though Reynaud sometimes made a pure Cuvée Syrah. That, too, I tasted – it was wonderful but unobtainable.

Both Rayas and Fonsalette were essentially single vineyard wines (though Fonsalette might occasionally include rejected components of Rayas) but Pignan was a puzzle. 'What goes into it?' There was a pause. 'Oh, the less good wines of Rayas and some other things, it's a secret.' When I pressed him for a clue, he whispered in my ear – that his vineyard at Courthezon produced wonderful Grenache.

As for the whites, I was told that the 1991 Rayas was made from Grenache Blanc and Clairette; the Fonsalette from Grenache Blanc, Clairette, Chardonnay and Marsanne. Whether that was true and whether it applied in other vintages, heaven knows.

By all the rules most of these wines should have been undrinkable – I have never seen scruffier cellars – and rumour had it that mistakes were made and that a great deal of the production had to be discarded. But the best wines were magnificent – beautifully fine-textured reds with an unmatched autumnal splendour, and deep-coloured, old-fashioned whites with startling complexity, aromas of straw and quinces.

Rare, wonderful – and a mystery, like the man himself.

Muttering a private shorthand to his sister, gazing mournfully at his dogs, exercising some unspoken control over his labourers and smiling diffidently at visitors, Jacques Reynaud was unfathomable. I had the impression of an ancient child, sleepwalking through a hostile world and somehow surviving – and that at the heart of all his peculiarities there was an innocence, untouched.

It is said that he died while buying a new pair of shoes.

1979/1994

Un Train Peut en Cacher un Autre

As you hesitate at any railway crossing in rural France you may notice a small enamelled sign proclaiming these mysterious words – Un train peut en cacher un autre. The phrase has become so embedded in the French language that it no longer needs explanation, but if you are very lucky you might come across a rare example of the full-colour original from the 1930s, a graphic masterpiece. In this version the warning not to cross without looking both ways is reinforced by a plaintive scene of a woman standing beside a stationary train, babe in arms and child tugging at her skirt, as her husband falls backwards in front of her, having been hit by an express coming in the opposite direction. Un train peut en cacher un autre. One train can hide another.

It is one of my favourite proverbs.

1973

Cherasco, Waiting for a Hero

The Piemontese countryman may be short, weather-beaten and shabbily dressed, but his self-esteem is worthy of Napoleon. With stubborn conviction he proclaims that Barolo is the wine of kings and demands an emperor's ransom for a few pungent knobbles of white truffle.

Such pride finds expression as best it can. The traditional peasant family of the Langhe hills, in northwest Italy, eats and entertains in a front room that is fitted out with the latest kitchen units and equipment, regardless of expense; but the oven is used as a cupboard and the fridge holds a single bottle of grappa. All the cooking is done at the back, hidden from view, on a primitive wood-burning stove; the front room is for show.

The riddle of this double kitchen, the relationship between truth and gesture, is a peculiarly Piemontese enigma which combines the desire for display with a love of secrecy. I am reminded of such ambiguities when I visit Cherasco.

Perched on a high plateau in Piemonte, above the confluence of the rivers Tanaro and Stura, Cherasco has an air of surreal mystery and silent rhetoric, as if waiting for Fellini. Streets intersect at right angles and stretch towards the vanishing point; heroic monuments are constructed like painted scenery; shuttered facades hide gorgeously decorated rooms, inhabited by ghosts. Cherasco is a film set, abandoned in the eighteenth century.

Such complex artifice seems disproportionate to the scale of the place. So does its name Citta di Cherasco. But the Italian concept of 'city' (smaller than ours) is resonant with pretensions to grandeur, based on history and pride.

All the other hill villages of this region have twisting medieval street plans of organic complexity, winding round church and castello, within the strong walls that were designed to safeguard their inhabitants, their cattle and their wine from the ruthless hordes of invaders. For this was the route from France, and the local dialect still reflects the endless switches of political allegiance that shaped the fortunes of these valleys and plains.

Cherasco is different, because it was founded on 12 November 1243 by the Marchese Manfredo Lancia (viceroy of the emperor Frederick Barbarossa) as a stronghold to guard the approaches to Alba. That purpose, and Cherasco's continuing strategic importance, imposed on the place a series of arbitrary forms, reflecting the changing fashions of military architects, obsessed with geometry. Their elaborate fortifications proved to be no more than a bombastic hoax (time and again the town surrendered without a fight) but each phase left traces, incongruous elements of a jumbled past: the medieval civic tower (rectangular column of brick, balanced on sturdy arches); the fourteenth-century Viscount's castle (as strongly fortified against attack from the town as it was against invasion from without); and a wide path which traces the now vanished circuit of seventeenth century bastions, designed by Antonio Vitozzi. Most remarkable of all is the absolute regularity of Cherasco's rectilinear plan.

I followed a funeral procession through these straight streets until we arrived in a tiny square in front of the church of San Pietro. The men stayed outside, chatting and smoking, while the women prayed for the deceased. I stayed, too, gazing up at the simple Romanesque façade, which is wonderfully adorned with green majolica plates, studding the brickwork like enamelled badges.

Then I stepped through the door and into another world; for San Pietro's interior was utterly remodelled in the seventeenth century. Cherasco skipped the Renaissance (Piemonte was riven by war) but found its perfect expressive form in the language of Italian baroque. This is the architecture of theatre, of splendid stage sets and heroic gestures, of flourishes so exuberant that you scarcely notice the lack of substance, of facades that gloriously evoke a third (or fourth) dimension, completed only in the imagination.

Such vistas and visions imply a point of view, an appropriate position for the spectator as much as for the object of his contemplation. In Cherasco it is the citizen who forms the centre of this world of illusion; the countryside is merely a backdrop, its inhabitants the stagehands.

Stand, for example, on Cherasco's main axis, the Via Vittorio Emanuele. This long, wide street is lined with palaces (the word 'palazzo' expresses much the same pretension as 'citta') that open onto derelict courtyards and overgrown gardens. Gothic arcades rub shoulders with classical porticos and pediments, and the modest shops of a country village are housed in these mutilated remnants of a grander age; but at either end of the street is a triumphal arch, closing the view with splendour.

One of these, the Porto Narzole, frames the abrupt transition between town and country. The outlines may be derived from Palladio or Vitruvius but it is little more than a brick wall pierced by arches, an elegant silhouette to be viewed at a distance, never close enough to reveal its construction. Sufficient detail has been added on the town side to lend conviction but as you approach from the country the wall is utterly unadorned. Pigeons nest in the holes that were left when its wooden scaffolding was removed, centuries ago.

That hasty sketch was roughed out by the set designer as an afterthought, to echo its much grander brother the Arco del Belvedere, which closes the opposite end of the vista. This splendid construction was designed by Giovenale Boetto as a votive to the Madonna, in thanksgiving for Cherasco's escape from the plague of 1630. Seen from the town it seems fully three-dimensional. Pillars flank the arches and support a massive cornice, on which stand dramatic statues of saints, gesturing to heaven. More saints (disguised as ancient Romans) gaze thoughtfully from the shelter of their niches at the traveller below. But ride through the central arch on your prancing stallion and look back over your shoulder. It's a fake, another stage set. The reverse of the arch is a plain, roughly stuccoed wall, leaning slightly outward and supported by buttresses; a theatrical prop, designed to impress.

Cherasco's immunity to a plague that devastated Piemonte (and much of the rest of Europe) had a powerful effect on its fortunes. The immediate consequence was that the town was chosen in 1631 as the healthiest place for peace negotiations, to end the war of Monferrato. Cherasco played host to plenipotentiaries of the kings of France and Spain, the Hapsburg Emperor and the Pope, the Dukes of Mantua and Monferrato. The papal legate was Giulio Mazzarino, a cunning young diplomat who later achieved notoriety in France as Cardinal Mazarin. Peace was signed and Cherasco flourished.

That prosperity was enhanced by the town's reputation for healthy air and good drainage. The peripatetic court of the Piemontese kings was often based here and all their hangers-on, nobles and clerics, wanted to build themselves a monument. Hence the spate of construction of churches and 'palaces', which give Cherasco today its agreeable air of decayed aristocracy.

All of which provided employment for Sebastiano Taricco, painter, architect, native of Cherasco and eventually its mayor. The most important secular buildings with which Taricco is associated are the Palazzo Salmatoris, in Via Emmanuelle, and the Palazzo Gotti di Salerno in Via Ospedale, in both of which he painted magnificent frescoes. The former is connected with all the great events of Cherasco's history (including those peace negotiations of 1631) while the latter is now the Museo Adriani, which was founded in the nineteenth century by an antiquarian obsessed with coins. It has a wonderfully carved front door, which seems perpetually closed; the museum is only open for an hour and a half in the morning, on the first Sunday of every month, and occasionally on Saturdays in summer. There is something quintessentially 'Cherascese' in that arbitrary indifference to visitors.

Taricco's work is more readily appreciated in his masterpiece, the Church of Santa Maria del Popolo, which was completed in 1709, a year before the architect's death. The façade is spectacular. Viewed down the narrow perspective of the Via Ospedale, it shimmers in the slanting light of a late afternoon like a mirage of splendour from another world, seeming closer and larger than reality; a theatrical thunderclap. The finest mellow brickwork replicates carved stone, forming pillars and pediments, architraves and cornices of extraordinary crispness and invigorating exuberance. Details are repeated on varying scales, and the entire façade is a triumph of baroque chiaroscuro. Above it hovers an octagonal cupola, lighter in colour, cunningly insubstantial.

The locked church doors are an extension of this stagecraft, suggesting an unseen vault of darkness pierced by shafts of light, with props and scaffolds supporting decayed splendour; a Piranesi engraving, swarming with bats. I was disappointed to learn from the only reliable guidebook that the reality is otherwise – the interior of Santa Maria del Populo has 'an effect of graceful exuberance, typical of eighteenth-century rococo'. I prefer my shadows, and Cherasco invites such dreams.

In the evening light, as Cherasco entered its long political decline, aristocratic ladies would display themselves on the beautiful balconies for which the town is famous. Exquisite silks (made in the Jewish ghetto, between Via Vittorio and

Via Ospedale) rustled against ironwork balustrades. They were waiting for a hero.

On 25 November 1796, Napoleon entered Cherasco at the head of a conquering army, and the ladies swooned. He installed himself at the Palazzo Salmatoris while dictating terms of surrender to the royal house of Savoy, but took time out, it is said, to plant a plane tree as a symbol of peace (a story almost no one believes) and to enjoy a snack of sweet almond cakes and Moscatel, prepared for him by one of the town's many convents. Two hundred years later I was told that he walked in this garden here, that he sipped his Moscatel over there.

There is another legend, probably invented, that a shady character approached Napoleon as he strolled in the streets of Cherasco and tried to sell him a white truffle. The Emperor reeled at the price, and for years afterwards would tell the story to his intimates, miming his shock with the conviction of a born actor and striking the famous attitude, immortalised in his portraits – hand on heart, pale and wan, expression like a glazed fish.

The Cherascese fell in love with Napoleon. Here was another short, absurdly self-confident man (just like themselves) who had risen from obscurity to emblazon his name across the world. The tiny Corsican's extraordinary powers of self-projection spanned the gap between reality and dreams, summarising all that the architecture of the place implies. He personified their pride, writ large.

But Cherasco was in decline. Palazzi were shoddily built and painted in trompe d'oeil, simulating the carved stonework that their owners could no longer afford; and gradually they stopped building at all. Impoverished and disillusioned, the nobility disappeared, leaving the town to others who lived like squatters in the decaying splendour of this extraordinary place. And so it remains. Cherasco today is a town of ghosts and memories.

Years ago I found myself sitting with family and friends in the faded elegance of the oldest restaurant in the town. We were the only customers. The aged proprietor served us course after course of classic Piemontese food, in dignified silence, but eventually he spoke, with the cracked voice of an oracle. 'Napoleon ate his first truffle in this place. It was the season of truffles when he visited us.'

1982

Home Winemaking
in Piemonte

Autumn in Piedmont is a marvellous time. The days are bright, the air is crisp and the vintage brings a feeling of satisfying activity. From early morning you come across piles of empty baskets or plastic boxes stacked beside the road, and groups of strong and cheerful women, ready to set to work. Later in the day the boxes (filled with grapes) will be lying in the shade of the vines, waiting to be loaded onto trucks and trailers, even the occasional ox-cart, and taken to the cantina. This may be a large cooperative, modern and well equipped, or the modest cellar of an individual grower. It seems that every farm has a barn with a few vats of fermenting must and on the back streets of every village the doors stand open. As you peer from the bright sunshine into the cool darkness of these unsuspected cantinas you can smell the fresh grape juice and watch the operations of primitive winemaking, essentially unchanged since medieval times.

On one such street in the hill village of Rocca Grimalda, high above Ovada, the pavement was blocked by a small old-fashioned basket press. Three elderly men were enjoying the sun as they squeezed the last juice out of the red grapes following the fermentation. Noticing my interest they invited me into the tiny cellar, brought out a bottle of the previous year's wine (with a handwritten label) and insisted that I taste the stuff. The labourer paused in his work at the press and the padrone and his friend beamed proudly as I muttered a wholly unmerited compliment on their homemade wine.

It was an entertaining and picturesque scene but it has to be admitted that the end result was almost undrinkable. There was little difference in scale, and none in basic technique, between their winemaking and that of the man I had come to see, whose equally simple cellar lay a few doors up the street. Yet their Dolcetto was the worst I have ever tasted, while his is by far the best.

Giuseppe Poggio is a perfectionist with the air of a village grocer. In his stained brown-coat he's the sort of man you'd expect to find behind the counter of an old-fashioned shop, selling everything from vegetables to horse liniment; the kindly old fellow who wraps up your bit of cheese with the smiling and courteous deference of one who knows that you won't find better quality in any of the fancy shops or flashy supermarkets.

But this modest man is, in his local way, quite famous. Anyone in the village will direct you to his house, and he carries off the most coveted prizes at the Asti wine fair. He is one of those small growers whose name, for enthusiasts of his region's wines, far exceeds his very limited production.

'My preoccupation is to make a good wine, not a lot of wine.' He points to the end of the little cellar: 'Look at this wall of bottles – all my production is there – it's a nice wall, eh?' He makes no more than 700 cases a year, almost all of them Dolcetto.

This, the 'little sweet', is a grape that appears to originate in Piedmont; one of the three varieties that produce all the notable red wines of this region. Nebbiolo makes the grand Barolo and the slightly less grand Barbaresco: wines that have a rich, autumnal complexity, a hint of tar and the capacity for long life. Barbera, highly prized locally, is the red equivalent of Bourgogne Aligoté – appetising but sometimes too astringent to the non-Italian palate. Dolcetto makes the quaffing wine, the Italian Beaujolais. It is normally drunk within a year or two of the vintage when you can relish its delicious immediacy, its mouthfilling flavour of ripe fruit which has a refreshing bitterness at the finish.

In Poggio's hands this grape is transformed to make a wine that has an extraordinary depth of character, a rich, almost chocolatey density of fruit, great length of flavour and the stamina to last well in bottle. He attributes a great deal of the quality to the situation of his vines, on the Trionzo hill. 'The wine there is special, it's something in the ground.' He has two vineyards on this rock, one facing south, the other northwest, a total of three hectares. The combination of grapes from both sides of the hill produces, he believes, a better-balanced wine.

There is nothing particularly unusual about the vinification of Poggio's Dolcetto unless you count his perfectionism and the fact that the miniature cement cubes in which the wine ferments are painted to resemble wooden botte; the large casks that are the source of Italy's vinous woes. The interesting thing is the maturation, which takes place in an extraordinary collection of small oak casks, too random in origin to be dignified with the title 'barriques'.

The question of 'barrique' versus 'botte' is a subject of much dispute in Italy. There is debate as to whether the small French-style cask is better than the big Germanic barrel, sometimes made of chestnut, sometimes oak. There is a considerable argument as to whether the smell and taste of new oak is a desirable ingredient in wine and there is a historical dispute: some growers, Poggio included, argue that prior to this century the Italians always used small casks for maturing the wine and that botte were only employed for fermentation. Above all, there are claims and counter-claims as to who, among the present generation of winemakers, was the first to experiment with barrique ageing.

Giuseppe Poggio is not one of the fashionable candidates in this contest but we may as well record that he bought his first barrique (actually a 200-litre cask of Slovenian oak) in the former Yugoslavia, in 1970. He's not a fan of new oak, much preferring the effect of second-hand casks, which he buys all over the place. The most unlikely item in his collection is a Scotch whisky cask, formerly a sherry hogshead, that he found in Genoa. It took him ages to get rid of the smell of whisky. He steamed the cask, rinsed it repeatedly with hot and cold water, and finally cured it with wine; Dolcetto, Malvoisie, Moscato and Barbera. It took over three weeks of continuous labour.

Most good winemakers have a few eccentric habits and Giuseppe Poggio is no exception. He thinks things out for himself, adapts the old traditions, and delights in astonishing the world with the results. Many well-qualified oenologists would refuse to believe that anything good could come out of such scruffy cellars and I have heard an American taster, furious at Poggio's haphazard indifference to hygienic theory, mutter crossly about residual sugar. But the fact of the matter is that he produces the best Dolcetto in Italy. His 'normal' quality was my idea of perfection until I realised that in exceptional vintages he produces minute quantities of something even more remarkable, his Riserva Speciale.

Having always thought that Dolcetto was his only love, it came as a slight shock to discover that he also plays around with Barbera. His version is dark in colour, with a slight prickle of gas, and has greater generosity than most specimens of this dour grape. Poggio's secret is to leave the lees of his Dolcetto in the vat and to ferment the Barbera on top. He claims this softens its natural astringency.

Giuseppe likes surprises. On my last visit he greeted me like a conjuror about to produce a wholly unexpected treat. We went upstairs to his house to sample the new vintage of Dolcetto, to munch a few grissini and haggle about prices. There on the table, the focus of all attention, was his little baby.

'I am now the only producer in the world of this wine.' Giuseppe Poggio untied the cunningly knotted string that held the cork in place and poured the bottle carefully, so as not to disturb the sediment, into half a dozen mismatched glasses. With the attentive air of a proud father he waited for our reaction.

It was delicious: green-gold in colour, scented of honey and elderflowers, gently effervescent. The flavour of ripe greengages was given life and definition by fresh acidity and a marvellously invigorating bitterness at the finish. Poggio was delighted at our enthusiasm. A smile and a nod, a little clearing of the throat. As he topped up our glasses it was clear that this bottle-fermented sparkler had not been disgorged, for there was sediment at the bottom of the bottle and the wine was now slightly cloudy. Realising that we liked it, Poggio became voluble with enthusiasm.

He explained its history. Years ago, this *spumante* was something of a local speciality, made by most of the local growers. Production gradually died out and even the name of the grape variety was forgotten. Only an obscure nickname survived: *Kari-ja L'Osü*, the ass's burden.

That is Piemontese dialect. The Italian translation, Carica l'Asino, is what appears on the hand-drawn, photocopied label that adorns Giuseppe's bottle, together with the words 'Vino Raro'.

Rare indeed. Poggio has only been making the wine since 1981 and he is the last producer, working from a few unreliable scraps of the old traditions and using a great deal of his own winemaking intuition. He has at least managed to find a few rows of the old vines but they don't yield much. There's just enough juice to fill a small cask, sufficient to make 200 bottles if all goes well. He sells a few bottles locally but essentially it's home-made wine for enjoying with his friends.

There are moments when I wish I lived in one of those quiet, sunny streets of Rocca Grimalda, perched on its cliff in a remote corner of Piedmont. There is a timeless restfulness about the place and the local food is delicious: some of the best pasta in Italy, and, in the winter, the pungent magic of the white truffle. There would be the constant delight of being able to drop in on Giuseppe Poggio for a glass of Dolcetto, or Barbera, or of Carica l'Asino, the rarest wine in the world. Then I realise that it would also be necessary, from time to time, to take a glass of wine with his neighbours; and the memory of what *they* produce is sufficiently awful to cause me to rejoice in the bleak reality of a February day in east Suffolk. Winemaking, on the whole, is best left to professionals.

1986

La Rosa e il Leone

La Rosa & il Leone is hard to find, hidden behind a high wall and tall iron gate at the edge of the village of Colognola ai Colli – but when the gate creaks open you catch the first glimpse of a romantic, overgrown garden, filled with trees and columns and ruins and flowers, and then you discover that the garden is shared by two nineteenth-century houses, in one of which the sisters live and the other of which is occupied by their guests.

Their father (an industrialist from Verona who died in his fifties) bought the house that we stayed in as a place to escape the women of his family and immerse himself in his books. When his wife protested, he bought the house next door and created for her this elaborate garden – and also, seemingly by chance, acquired two small vineyards; one across the road from the house and one at the bottom of the garden. After his death the sisters remained here, not knowing what to do with his house until they hit upon the notion of offering its three spacious bedrooms to those, like us, looking for somewhere interesting to stay.

So we slept in luxury between the finest linen sheets (that had once formed part of their mother's dowry), took breakfast overlooking the garden and began to explore.

There were terraces and steps, a statue of a god abducting a plump nymph (offering rather token resistance), an elaborate ornamental pool, with irrigation channels branching off to various corners of the garden, now ruined and dry. Beyond was a cluster of fine cedars, on whose spreading branches my laundered shirts were hung to dry, splashes of bright blue in the shadows. A line of clouded glass windows, all open at the same angle, reflected a hallucinatory milky light into the old limonaia – where pots of lemon trees were brought inside in the winter. An ancient scythe hung from the wall of a tool shed, alongside a couple of hoes, a wooden hay rake and a shovel with the long handle and heart-shaped blade peculiar to Mediterranean countries. Swallows nested under the eaves. A path led to the vegetable patch, below which was a sunken lane and a wide landscape of vines, meadows, cypress and poplars.

The garden was sheltered from the road by a long wall, punctuated by niches in which pale nymphs danced soundlessly. There were pots of oleanders, a pomegranate. A winged Venetian lion guarded an arcade of twisted Veronese columns, shading a table at which sat one of the sisters, Giovanna, helping a small boy with his schoolwork, while his mother was busy sweeping the kitchen. It reminded me of those glimpses of domestic life in the paintings of Pieter de Hooch. There was a sense of timelessness.

But that apparent serenity concealed a more poignant history, slowly revealed to us by Giovanna and her sister Valeria.

Their father, it seems, had been a man of rigid authority, with a fixed view of women's place in the world. He deemed it shameful for his daughters to think of any career other than marriage – but had discouraged potential suitors. Valeria, when young, had a passion for ballet and was indeed so gifted that she was offered a place at La Scala, as a professional. Her father refused his consent, and by the time he died it was too late. Giovanna was in love. But the man could not wait indefinitely for parental approval. Another sister managed to escape the family history, married and went to live in the city. But Giovanna and Valeria remain, in what may seem a paradise to visitors but must, for them, be filled with thoughts of a life that has passed them by.

One afternoon I decided to explore the large house where we were staying, from top to bottom. It was light-filled but coolly grand – lots of marble, ponderous fireplaces – a nineteenth-century evocation of an imagined past, Romeo and Juliet. A flight of stairs led down to a semi-basement, which was how I discovered the cache of wine – and another story emerged.

I knew that the name of the place had been intended to honour the sisters' parents (his Lion of Venice, her Rose of Lombardy) so when I found a book, *La Rosa e il Leone*, lying on a desk near the wine, I picked it up expecting to learn more about their history. Instead, I found myself reading about Rosa Luxemburg and Leon Trotsky, and realised that Valeria was a frustrated revolutionary. This frustration, and a longing to find her own way of doing things, had finally found an outlet when she became a winemaker.

In 2004 Valeria decided that the sisters should no longer sell their grapes to the local Soave co-operative and for three consecutive glorious vintages, until the labour became too much for her, she selected the best, late harvested bunches, which she dried on racks for several weeks until the sugars were concentrated, the flavours complex and it was time to crush and ferment them. Valeria had the help of a local oenologist, but she followed, almost step by step, the instructions of the sixth-century agriculturist, Cassiodorus. It was he who first delimited and regulated the vineyards of Soave, and it is in his honour that Valeria named her wine, Cassiodoro. She even designed a very stylish label.

But that was that – for Valeria had no means of selling the Recioto that she had so lovingly made, apart from a few cases in her immediate locality. There it stayed, slowly maturing, in a cool room at the bottom of her father's house, until I discovered it – and took my first sip, in that beautiful ghost of a garden.

The most enticing apricot gold; aromas of conserved fruit, angelica, honey; flavours that combined a luscious, lingering sweetness with delicious fruit acidity. This was a wine to sip with toasted almonds, savour with desserts, relish on its own.

So then the negotiations began. Valeria agreed an astonishingly generous price. My former employers were persuaded to arrange a shipment. I wrote a leaflet extolling its wonders. The wine sold out within weeks.

It was recognition, at last, for a heroine.

2009

Lerma, Castille

A vast, sloping, empty square, grey cobbles. Lowering against a grey sky, the former Ducal palace – huge, abandoned, empty – inhabited only by thousands of swifts and swallows and martins which fill the air and dart through broken windows into the dark, grand, ruined splendour within.

Nearby an ancient convent – the enclosed order of Santa Clara – and a fortress church, dedicated to San Pedro, to which the nuns have access via a screened-off gallery at the rear. One of them is playing the organ as I enter and peers down curiously at me through the protection of a huge iron grille, covered in fearsome spikes, to guard against infidels. Or men. Sad sense of stillness, the self-imposed life sentence. All the windows of the convent are covered in wooden lattices which give only the tiniest glimpse for those within of a strolling, changing world that they can never re-enter.

In the days of its pomp, three hundred years ago, there were six convents in this small hilltop town, south of Burgos. Now there may be half a dozen nuns. And thousands of swifts and swallows and martins.

1995

In Search of Juan Garcia

Heading west from Zamora we passed through an ancient land of stone-walled fields and green lanes, cañadas reales, which shepherds use to herd their flocks, migrating each spring and autumn; a neolithic stone circle in a green meadow; a landscape of giant granite slabs, lying together like sleeping prehistoric elephants. As evening fell we turned off the narrow road onto a rutted track and drove across a rocky upland. We wound down the windows. The air was dense with the aromas of camomile, thyme and evergreen oak, the resinous scent of cistus and the sweetness of wild roses and honeysuckle. Occasionally I could hear the gentle clangour of goat bells or the clopping of mules, coming home from the fields, but there was a rich, velvety stillness, the silence of another time. Eventually we reached the village, a place that had only recently discovered electricity and where the only visitors were ornithologists.

Telmo Rodriguez and I were on one of our annual expeditions to explore the forgotten wine regions of Spain, in the hope of discovering some special combination of grape variety and vineyard that might provide an opportunity to re-invent a local winemaking tradition. Earlier that day we had stopped at an oenological research station in Rueda, to taste a cross-section of the region's autochthonous grapes. One of them held our attention, with a fresh, appetising astringency, a hint of damsons. It was said to be thin-skinned, agreeable in good years but prone to rot in wet weather. It was called Juan Garcia.

We were told that it survived in a few half-abandoned vineyards, further west, close to the Portuguese border, near a place called Fornillos. And that was all.

This was where we arrived, in the dusk. A huge mulberry tree loomed beside an austere stone church, an old woman was herding home her goats, an unusually fine mule was tethered near a stone well in the middle of the village. When a man came to unhitch the mule we asked whether he knew anything about the local grape variety, Juan Garcia. 'Someone who knows will be along shortly', was the enigmatic reply. How can we recognise him?' 'He's the only man in the village with a car.'

So we waited, as it grew darker. A few cattle, lumbering primaeval beasts, loomed out of the gloom and padded by, unaccompanied. A couple of women, side-saddle on mules, trotted down the unsurfaced lane. And then, just as we were losing hope, we saw the headlights of a car and heard the rattle as it came closer. Telmo stood in the middle of the track and waved it to a stop. Leaning through the window, he began an animated conversation with the driver.

This was indeed 'the man who knows' – a local vigneron called Tomas Corral. He told us that our elusive grape grew a bit further west, close to the river Duero along the border with Portugal. He drew us a little map of all the surrounding villages, on the back of a voting slip for the local elections. He marked directions to the Casa Persianas Verdes (House of the Green Shutters), where we might be able to stay, and to a nearby bar, where we could eat. He knew everything we needed.

The following day we went to explore the scrubland plateau and the steep slopes of the river gorge. We found tiny fields surrounded by stone walls built of large triangular slabs, infilled with piles of rubble. Red earth speckled with glints of mica, schist and black marble. Each little vineyard had a small stone hut in the corner, the Caseta de Viña, for the workers to shelter and store their tools. There were no gates. To gain access the famers dismantled a section of wall and rebuilt it afterwards – or stopped the gap with a bundle of thorn bushes.

Oleander, cistus, broom, cork oak, evergreen oak, olive trees. The oaks were low and spreading, and pigs used to feed on their acorns. Now the pigs are gone.

The next village, Pinilla, was a quiet and peaceful place – pots of geraniums on windowsills, an old man sitting in the sun. A small stone-walled patch was filled with ripe wheat – not one of the short modern varieties, bred for the combine harvester, but some ancient strain – thin straw like very tall grass, small ears and grains, irregular in height. A man and his wife, dark and stocky, were moving slowly and steadily, harvesting the crop with iron sickles and laying it in small bundles, before tying the bundles and stacking them in a single stook, like a tiny haystack. The woman was dressed in black, as they all were.

In a nearby yard what looked like a wooden sled was propped against the wall. The base was scored with grooves, into which were slotted sharp stone shards. Laden with a heavy rock and drawn by a donkey, it had been used until a year or two earlier to thresh the wheat from the straw, spread over the floor of the yard.

Almond trees, a few walnuts, sweet chestnuts. A man riding on a donkey, his wife walking behind. The ruin of a car, rusting in the corner of an abandoned vineyard, with scorched and yellowing grass growing up through the chassis and around the black stumps of dead vines. We passed the municipal refuse cart, drawn by a mule, and another mule dragging a wooden plough with a single tine – like those depicted in medieval illuminations. A man was drawing water from a well to irrigate his vegetable garden, using a long pole pivoting on the fork of a tall post – with a heavy stone lashed on one end, the rope and bucket suspended from the other – rocking up and down, perfectly counter-balanced, in the rhythms of an agriculture unchanged for thousands of years. A breath-taking pause in time.

An old woman was standing in the archway of her tiny, black cellar in Fermoselle, where the wine was fermented and stored in granite tanks. We asked what grapes she used. 'Malvasia, tinto this, tinto that, Juan Garcia . . . I don't really know, they're all mixed up in the vineyard.' The wine was clean, appetising (surprisingly so in such primitive cellars) but very light in colour, despite the red grapes.

We visited the cellars of a couple of local co-operatives, one stinking and dirty, the other clean and well-equipped with stainless steel tanks and presses – but in both cases the scale of the tanks was utterly disproportionate to the tiny local vineyards. Any individuality of place, grape variety or grower was submerged in the communal soup.

One of the local growers made decent but forgettable wine in underground tanks lined with a crazy assortment of tiles, bought as job lots. Another offered us his version of vermouth, made to a recipe that he wouldn't even tell his sons, and a red wine that had been in bottle for fourteen years – now almost amber in colour and well on its way to wine vinegar. He asked what we thought of it. 'Very interesting' was my reply.

We went to the river and crossed over the dam into Portugal, and into another century, almost like the present day. The cheerful, whitewashed town of Miranda do Douro, very clean, lots of flowerpots and cats, was centred on a square with a little church, filled with painted and gilded reliefs of saints and martyrs and Madonnas, and a madly exuberant vision of the Last Judgement.

From a quayside on the Douro (the spelling of the river changes on each side of the border) we took a boat upstream, watching eagles and buzzards and vultures soaring above us. Unnoticed except by me, a swallowtail butterfly fluttered through the boat.

On the way back east, we stopped once more in Fornillos, because we had heard rumours of a cheesemaker in the village and went to investigate. Nothing prepared us for what we found, for the cheesemaker was an Irish girl.

Sara from southern Ireland had married Patxi from northern Spain, having met at Salamanca university. Together they settled in this remote place, where they constructed an impeccable, tiny dairy within one of the old, stone-walled houses, and began to make wonderful cheese, which they named La Setera, after a brook that runs from the village through the pastures of their goats.

This much we discovered as we talked to them and tasted the cheese – but we also learnt that the yield of goat's milk was very seasonal; from October to December cheese production ceased. Telmo and I had the same thought simultaneously – that here was someone, trained in hygiene and temperature control, short of work around vintage time; a perfect wine-maker in waiting.

So Telmo rented a stone house nearby, installed a couple of small stainless-steel tanks, and persuaded Sara to help make an experimental batch of Juan Garcia. They kept in constant touch by mobile phone. When the fermentation was complete, Telmo arranged for the wine to be brought to his own cellars, for further ageing in cask.

Six months later I tasted the result. The wine was dull, tough and lacking all that we had hoped for. Telmo tried once again, but then moved on to other projects, convinced that Juan Garcia could not be revived. It seemed the end of a great adventure.

Nine years passed and then suddenly, in the autumn of 2004, some samples arrived at my office and I discovered, to my amazement, that Sara and Patxi had refused to accept defeat. They had researched the area, identified the best plots of Juan Garcia, built the trust of growers who were prepared to work with them and constructed their own small winery. It was ready just in time for the 2003 vintage. When the wines were bottled, they made contact.

Those first samples already showed promise and the following vintage was good enough for export – a trio of wines, each of them delicious: red and rosado from Juan Garcia (ancient vines, up to a century old) and a white from Malvasia. They were named, like the cheese, La Setera.

Tasting these wines, I felt my heart lift. The Tinto Joven (young red) was deep purple, with aromas of plums, sloes and blackberries, brambly fruit flavours and a rustic earthiness at the finish – and the white was characterful, delightfully crisp. But the real star was the Rosado. Lurid pink, hints of red fruit (raspberries, cranberries, cherries), gently tannic, appetising and delicious with food. In this wine, most unexpectedly, Juan Garcia had achieved its apotheosis. It seemed like a miracle.

I ordered a shipment and drank the Rosado all summer long. In celebration.

1995/2005

Aguas de Toledo

As we crested the hill and came around a bend in the road, Toledo lay before us – a huddle of stone buildings perched on a great rock, encircled by the river Tagus, deep in its gorge. This was El Greco's view, but warmer, glowing in the slanting sun of late afternoon rather than glistening under a lurid sky on the brink of a storm. And there beside the road was a motorcycle, lying in the twentieth-century dust, and its rider, beckoning us to stop.

My father pulled our Bedford van onto the verge. A brief conversation, mostly in gestures, ended in the motorcyclist hitching a lift with us into the city, to find a friend who would collect the broken-down bike and take it back to be repaired. When we arrived at the garage he was effusive in his gratitude but repetitions of the words 'Fábrica de Espadas' left us perplexed. It was only with the help of his friend that we eventually realised this meant the Royal Sword Factory, where the motorcyclist worked, and that we were invited to meet him there in the morning for a private tour. He wrote his name and the address on a scrap of paper and waved us farewell as we headed back to the Parador, overlooking the city.

I was thirteen years old. The lightning strokes of colour in El Greco's paintings and the flashing of Toledo blades swirled in my head as I stood on the terrace of the hotel, gazing at the gorge, lost in an imagined past.

In the morning we found our way to the factory – a cluster of long brick buildings, close to the river. Toledo blades had been famous for more than a thousand years – hot steel tempered in the cold waters of the Tagus, an elemental, almost magical process – but when the Real Fabrica de Espadas was founded, in 1761, it was already near the end for battles fought with swords. By the time of our visit most of the factory was closed and the remaining workshops were making weapons of pompous formality – swords for officers with gilded hilts and heavy tassels. Only afterwards, when I bought a dangerous flick knife at a hardware store in the city, did it seem that an ancient tradition was still alive – 'of cutting foreign throats, of breaches, ambuscadoes, Spanish blades'.

Mercutio's words in *Romeo & Juliet* match this city of chiaroscuro, a place of dark alleys, slants of dazzling sunshine, closed convents and elaborate iron grilles in the dim interiors of baroque churches. That sense of drama, bordering on violence – memories of the Inquisition – is echoed by the pale faces and black cloaks crowding around the corpse of a man in gleaming armour, as he is lowered into his tomb by figures clad in gold. *The Burial of Count Orgaz* is one of two great masterpieces by El Greco that symbolise the city – the other being his storm-lit *View of Toledo* – a work so powerful that it shapes our sense of the physical reality.

Each of us thinks that we see his view as we look across the gorge, but El Greco has tricked us, shifting the cathedral to make a better composition, emptying the landscape of extraneous detail, exaggerating the depth of the ravine. It's a theatrical vision that somehow distils the real place. But when I visited Toledo for the second time, more than half a century later, my gaze was caught by small, almost unnoticeable things – roots of plants bursting through steps leading down from the city to the gorge, graffiti on a medieval door, iron rectangles embedded in the cobbled streets, embossed with the words 'Aguas de Toledo', 'Agua Potabile', 'Tagus'. The Rio Tajo is the city's water supply, a constant, subliminal presence as you walk through these alleys, threading beneath your feet and casting subtle reflections of light from far below. Down in its gorge, almost encircling the city, the river is alive with drama, foaming violently through channels that once led to turbines, tumbling over a weir and spreading in broad shallows, with the sudden gleam of a kingfisher flashing low across the current.

Roots, water, steel, sunlight and shadows – all these elements are entwined in the work of Cristina Iglesias – the most recent artist to have expressed Toledo's essence in ways that make us rethink our image of the city. Tres Aguas – three waters – is the name of her mesmerising project, completed in 2014.

Walking along the edge of the river to the old sword factory, with Iglesias and a group of friends, I felt a strange overlapping of time. It seemed for a moment that I was following the footsteps of my childhood, but then I realised I had never trodden so close to the water, splashed by the spray as it hurtled through a rusting mill-race, smelling the plants and the mud of the riverbank. Nor had I noticed the elegant tower that was our first destination, built of buff-coloured brick in restrained mudéjar style, discreetly renovated.

It is an old water tower, and the tanks are still there at the top, as we discovered when we climbed a flight of stairs on the outside of the building. Water from the river had been pumped up here, to be stored until released in a rush into channels in the nearby factory, to temper the steel blades that were forged down below. But the factory closed in the 1970s and the tanks were empty.

The original windows have been replaced by thin sheets of alabaster, filtering the light so that the empty interior space has a calm, reflective character as we gaze down from high above. And then I realise that it is reflective in a literal sense, for those milky windows, brick walls and the iron stairs that descend within the building are repeated in disorienting perspective on the surface of a shallow pool that fills the base of the tower. The surface stirs, reflections shift, and a tangle of roots is revealed as the water imperceptibly drains away. It is as if the river itself momentarily ran dry, for the base of this pool is cast in metal the colour of greenish mud, a complex relief of decaying vegetation, leaves and stems, like the bed of the Tagus itself.

Slowly, silently, the pool fills again, pauses, and empties. It's hypnotic. I descend the stair, stand by the water's edge and find my childhood memories flooding back – stamping through the sky's reflection in a puddle and gazing into local streams, hoping to see fish wriggling in the shadows.

Outside, in bright sunlight, we move on – all of us quiet, reflective – along the river and up to the city, through dark alleys, past an ancient graffitied door and a window blocked by thin sheets of tin, pierced with holes like the grille of a confessional. I glance down and spot one of those small cast-iron reminders that the river has risen and runs under our feet, in a labyrinth through the city. Aguas de Toledo.

The second of the 'Three Waters' is located in a convent. Up a few stone steps, twisting past heavy wooden screens, rusty red, I am reminded that this was an enclosed order of nuns who never made contact with the world except through a lattice. Into a small room, a former cell, with a couple of simple concrete benches along the walls. A pool, half seen in the shadows, is silently filling and emptying, filling and emptying, above its bed of roots and leaves.

Cristina Iglesias made those screens to echo the barricades in churches and convents that formerly imprisoned nuns as the brides of Christ. But she has also evoked the elaborate piercings and patterns of Moorish architecture (the alternative, Islamic history of Spain) and the grilles of Jewish synagogues – all those religions that once co-existed in Toledo. Further, unexpected layers of history are embedded in her creation, for the next day I discovered the extraordinary Art Deco screens in the ticket hall of the train station, which opened in 1919. Here, in brilliant exuberance, repeated again and again, are the traditional motifs that Iglesias reworked, made weighty, sombre, seemingly cast in red iron. Her screens are barriers, keepers of secrets, as they protect the pool in the Convent of Saint Clara.

This pool, the smallest and most private of the Tres Aguas, is the one that enforces silence on its watchers, as if the convent's rules, forbidding speech, still held sway. It is a space of contemplation.

The third water, the largest, is also the noisiest, because it slants across the pavement in Toledo's busiest square, the Plaza del Ayuntamiento, in front of the grand city hall and facing the cathedral. But the noise is muted, for the filling and emptying of this great pool is almost silent, imperceptible, and the crowds slow down, pause to watch, as children dip toes and fingers in the water. Here, at the heart of the city, in its most evidently civic space, we can recover the pleasure of wandering along the riverbank, gazing at roots in the mud. It's as if the country has invaded the city – except that one of the great urban pleasures, watching other people, is doubled as we stand there, looking at reflections in the water. Their images shiver, dissolve, reform as the cycle continues, and as people drift away or come closer, drawn irresistibly to the repetitions of flux and ebb, flux and ebb.

Perfectly rectangular, this pool breaks the formal symmetry of its location by lying at a slant to the facade of the city hall – a long diagonal of water, at once calming and surprising. It redefines its space.

So, too, with each of the 'Three Waters'. Walking along the river, up through the city, experiencing these serene pools in locations both public and private is a meditative act, like the routes of pilgrimage. It's a way of exploring Toledo, a passage through space and time that modifies our sense of the city, a work of art in which we are the participants. The fierce dramas of Toledo's past, visions of El Greco, mighty rock above the river's gorge, shafts of light, dark shadows, memories of the Inquisition, blades of tempered steel, civil war, noise of traffic, crowds of tourists – all is calmed. Hypnotised by water.

2015

Sounds of Istanbul

A wonderful photograph caught my eye today, while reading a newspaper. A black-haired girl staring at the camera – only her eyes and the top of her head visible in the frame – and behind her, resting on a pavement, two men and nine sheep, one of them black. Each man had an almost empty glass of tea on a saucer beside him. It was captioned Istanbul, 2019 by Emre Çakmak.

I hardly noticed the girl because ten years earlier I, too, had been mesmerised by the sight of sheep in the heart of this ancient city, and had snapped an old man casually prodding his tiny flock up a narrow street, oblivious to traffic. Looking afresh at that old photo, I counted the sheep. Once again there were nine, one of them black.

This surreal coincidence prompted me to return to Çakmak's image and face the girl's insistent gaze. Only then did I realise the strangest thing about it, that one of her eyes was blue, the other black.

Inexplicable wonders form the essence of this city. Two vast heads of Medusa, carved in classical times, were re-used – one upside down and one on its side – as the bases for columns in the Basilica Cistern, built by the Emperor Justinian in 532. A Bulgarian Orthodox church was assembled from cast iron components prefabricated in Vienna in the nineteenth century. English grandfather clocks with Arabic faces stand silent in many of the mosques. Such things echo the changing names for the place – Byzantium, Constantinople, Istanbul – evoking an extraordinary palimpsest of history, layer upon layer, shaping its form and meaning.

But what sticks in my mind are the smells, the tastes, the sights and sounds of immediate experience.

Even from my first visit, over fifty years ago, what I recall most vividly are the mournful sirens of the ferry boats as they set off across the Bosphorus for Asiatic Turkey. Now my memories of the city are crowded with smaller sounds – the thrumming of wind in the fishing lines stretched from the Galata Bridge, the slapping of water against wooden piles, the bell of the ancient tram, the Taksim Tunel, as it climbs the steep slope from the bridge towards the heart of the modern city. A latter-day scribe, sitting on a bench in a square, writes a formal letter on a portable typewriter, while his clients dictate to him. The clicking of the keys, the tinny cling at the end of each line, can just be heard above the noise of traffic. In a café near the Orthodox Patriarchate a couple of policemen play cards, slapping them down on the table. At another café, at an old madrasa which now serves as a carpet bazaar, a line of men seated on benches enjoy an aromatic smoke while catching up with the day's events, to the background rustle of newspapers and the quiet bubbling of water pipes. Everywhere in the oldest, most decrepit part of the city there are cats, which suddenly spit and squall as they fight with a rival.

I take a boat trip up the Bosphorus, to admire the beautiful wooden yali, the old summer residences of the rich, which line the shores as we pass. My ear is caught by the rhythms of conversation between two old men, sitting together on a bench. They make an engaging and somewhat unexpected couple. One wears a dark suit and black tie, neatly trimmed white moustache, a slightly formal air. The other seems more raffish, more intellectual, with long grey locks resting on the collar of his warm coat, a black and white scarf loosely knotted round his neck. Their talk is eager, engaged, and continues almost without pause as we sail slowly on. It forms a quietly enjoyable undertone to the noises of the boat and the bustle of passengers as we stop at various landing stages on the way north. I am so intrigued that eventually I tell them what a pleasure it is to listen to them, and then I learn that they met a few years earlier when their children (now married) were courting. Almost by chance they became friends, and now take this boat trip up and down the Bosphorus every few weeks, simply to have a chance of sitting on the deck in the sun, chatting together, at ease. They smile, we shake hands, and as I move a little further off the conversation resumes, the unhurried twining of different voices, a sort of music.

Memories of roasting chestnuts, or the rich aromas of the spice market, whet my appetite. I want to head down to Balikci Sabahattin for the most delicious fish, served in an atmosphere of near mayhem, or meander through the side streets to the slot in the wall where Osman Yüce makes the best rice pudding in Istanbul. But what I really long for is a simit.

These are the Turkish version of bagels, a twisted ring of gently chewy dough, sprinkled with sesame seeds. Described like that, it doesn't sound much, but this is the ubiquitous street food of Istanbul, served by itinerant vendors carrying a couple of dozen simits threaded on a pole, or with wooden tripods balanced on their heads, piled with fresh simits. That freshness is the secret, because simits are baked throughout the day, and should still be faintly warm from the oven when you take a bite.

A few moments before I left Istanbul for what proved the final time a vendor appeared, an old man, immaculate, a trayful of simits on his head. I bought one, my last taste of the city. As I turned away, having thanked him, I heard once again the characteristic cry, 'Nefis Simit, Simit' (exquisite simits) – with the last syllable of the word long drawn out, quavering, echoing down the street, fainter and fainter. Farewell.

2008

Footprint in the Sand

Essaouira – all the vowels in a word. It's like the echo of some imagined place, far away and long ago, or the rippling of tiny waves, faintly phosphorescent, as the receding tide slides over the sand, in the dusk. Even when it is rough and waves are crashing on the island of Mogador, which guards the bay, the shore of the coast can be calm.

The rocks of that island were harvested, two thousand years ago, for the shells of sea snails, murex – source of the Tyrian purple dye which stained the senatorial togas of ancient Rome. The Romans left and the natural harbour of the bay remained undisturbed for centuries, except by merchants who used it as a base to export molasses and sugar, and pirates who went marauding, to capture European slaves.

Then, in the middle of the eighteenth century, a Moroccan king decided to build a city, an Atlantic port, and employed

European architects to make his dream come true. The result is a curious mixture of Moorish tradition (narrow streets lined with secretive courtyard houses, hidden behind blank façades) and military fortifications that may once have seemed formidable but now have a charming, make-believe air.

The haven, for example, is protected by an elegant citadel (built by the Genoese) and fortified stone groins, constructed by a 'renegade Englishman', Ahmed el Inglizi. Bronze cannon poke from the embrasures of these harbour walls, adding to the illusion that this is someone's childhood memory, playing at pirates.

Outside the city the dusty land is dotted with scrawny argan trees, whose leaves form a 'pasture in the air' for local goats, which climb the trees and perch incongruously on their branches. It seems a hallucination.

'It is an ancient Mariner, and he stoppeth one of three.' Coleridge's clinging storyteller is suddenly beside me, in the form of a short, garrulous fisherman, named Abdul, who somehow inveigles himself into conversation with me and Irène as we stroll around the harbour, admiring the great sardine boats being built and repaired, and the smaller boats, crowding the moorings, which catch everything from anchovies to sharks. Abdul hauls out a well-thumbed sketchbook, filled with colourful drawings of fishermen and their catch, as he lures me into his net. I am his morning catch and must pay a few coins to escape.

Other transactions are happening around us, as coins are swapped for a bag of fish or eels. A box of hake and a couple of large rays lie on the quayside, waiting for a buyer.

Blue floats are woven into the edges of the fishing nets and the blue of the sea and the sky is echoed in the colour of small boats and sheds, fences and stalls, and within the Medina itself. Ancient doors and shutters, azure on whitewash, and each tiny shop in the market – everything is painted the same brilliant blue. The colour contrasts are dazzling. A blue-rimmed plate of pale green 'figs', slashed to show the bright red flesh inside – a speciality of Essaouira, conjured out of marzipan. Three bright oranges, perched on tagine lids, are displayed above three piles of oranges, framed in blue. Bunches of yellow bananas hang on a pinkish wall, splashed with blue, above a gaudy display of shining peppers (red, yellow, green), purple cabbages, and green heaps of parsley and coriander. Even the wooden reading desk in the Chaim Pinto synagogue (remnant of a vanished Jewish community that once accounted for nearly half the population of Essaouira) is painted this startling blue. We are shown around by the woman guardian, who treasures the place. She asks if I am Jewish. 'No. Are you?' She smiles, 'I'm Muslim.'

We eat lunch on the terrace of a busy seaside restaurant – grilled squid one day, tiny soles the next – as waves splash on the wall below our table. The smell of the sea.

Every evening I take a long walk around the bay, to the south of the town, as the receding tide patterns the sand in complex rhythms, leaving a pale, egg-shaped stone to gleam like a talisman from its tiny pool and a white feather to cast a long shadow in the slanting light. Those patterns are faint echoes of ripples, close to the town, but much more strongly marked the further I approach the rocks at the end of the bay.

The wide beach is very gently sloping, and the tide recedes a long way out, leaving a thin glaze of water to reflect the evening light. An old sailing vessel is moored on the horizon, near the 'Phoenician Island', behind which the sun is setting. Two tall fishing rods are propped in the shallows, their lines almost invisible as they stretch out to sea, with a man watching, hoping for the tug of a bite. Three dogs race across the wet beach and a young couple stands in chaste embrace, silhouetted against the sunset, doubled in their reflections on the strand.

The beach, at this time of day, is a place where boys and girls can meet unobserved by their parents, to chase each other through the shallows or write declarations of love, scratched in the sand, confident that the tide will erase their names (Amir + Fatima) before anyone reads and betrays them. As the light fades I see the veiled outline of a girl, crouched like a shadow by the tideline, tracing a heart with a stick. She leaves, the tide seeps in and within moments the heart is gently washed away. What remains, for a little while, is the faint outline of her sandal – its delicately pointed toe and the sharp indent of its heel.

2011

Paper Boats

Nebamun is hunting birds in the marshes of the Nile, standing astride on the deck of his small boat, his wife behind him and their daughter crouched between his splayed legs. His cat leaps in front to seize three of the waterfowl that spring from a thicket of papyrus. Beneath the boat the river teams with fish. Lotus flowers rise from the water and butterflies fill the air. It is a scene of abundance and happiness, an image of what Nebamun hoped for in the afterlife, 'enjoying himself and seeing beauty'.

Over three thousand years later and fifteen hundred kilometres upriver I, too, am seeing beauty, standing on the shore of Lake Tana (the largest in Ethiopia and source of the Blue Nile), as I watch a tiny, brightly coloured kingfisher, perched on a green stem of papyrus. Half a dozen small boats are crisscrossing the lake, so heavily laden with firewood that the men paddling them are almost under water. Others are fishing.

The past seems vividly present, for these boats are indistinguishable from that of Nebamun – made from bundles of papyrus lashed together with rope and tightly bound at each end, one pointed, one curved. No nails, no wood, and light enough for a man to carry. I found one, drying out after a fishing trip, propped upright against a tree on an island in the middle of the lake; the 'grain accountant' of Thebes would have known it at a glance.

Gazing once again at his tomb fresco (now in the British Museum) I noticed a small but important dissonance, between the brilliantly lifelike painting of cat, fish and birds, and the entirely schematic mode in which the cluster of papyrus is depicted. The reason is clear, for papyrus had long since been formalised as a hieroglyph – 'green/growth/vigour' – and had added symbolic resonance, recalling the primeval marshes of the creation myths and the papyrus pillars that were believed to hold up the sky. It had become impossible to paint in an entirely naturalistic way.

Papyrus is seemingly delicate but in fact remarkably tough, with pale green leaves (triangular in section) and distinctive fan-like fronds, and it was used by the ancient Egyptians in multiple ways. Paper was made of papyrus (as the entomology suggests). So, too, was the basket in which baby Moses was found by the Pharoah's daughter. So, too, were the earliest boats – a technique that was brought south to Lake Tana, three thousand years ago.

That sense of distant historic time is all pervasive in Ethiopia, but strangely ambiguous. The more it's talked about, the more you should be wary.

Ask the age of an ancient church or biblical manuscript

and you are likely to be told that it's from the fourth century, but most such claims are symbolic, not literal. The date has significance because it was then that the distinctively Ethiopian version of Christianity was adopted by the emperor Ezana – and from this time that the sacred texts were written in Ge'ez, a language that is now incomprehensible to most of the faithful including, I suspect, most priests.

This was true from the very beginning, so religious teaching was pictorial, not textual. The texts themselves were illustrated and the rock churches frescoed with cartoon strips of legend and scripture – painted in a formulaic but highly expressive style (strong outlines, vivid colours) that could still be legible in the dim light of the interiors. Colours fade, damp attacks the surface, so these paintings were constantly renewed, and in the process acquired a rich embroidery of legend. Vivid and wildly imagined, supplementing the original biblical narrative, fables of saints and miracles became embedded in the belief system of the faithful. Wondrous stories came to have the force of revelation.

Hence the accretions of myth surrounding the last Emperor, Haile Selassie, and his transfiguration in the legends of Rastafarianism. The Lion of Judah.

That highly coloured sense of historic continuity and religious legend pervades everyday life, especially outside the cities. The past is constantly present. Pilgrims trek for miles to a tiny, almost inaccessible church, Abuna Yemata Gah, carved into a vertical cliff, hundreds of metres above the valley floor. Crowds gather for a funeral, followed by a baptism, at Yeha – near the remains of a Sabaean temple, seventh century BC. The 'Jordan Laundry' ('we can clean any cloth') can be found near the 'Memory Bar' ('a place for husbands without wives') at the New Jerusalem of Lalibela, where clusters of subterranean churches were carved at laborious cost in the thirteenth century, deep in the rock. One of them was supposedly built overnight, by angels.

But historic memory is also embedded in the rituals of daily life, in this poor, arid, agricultural land. These memories are wordless, constantly re-enacted, unmodified by fable and superstition. Teams of oxen are driven in circles around a threshing floor, to separate grain from straw on a windy day, as dust rises and men toss the beaten straw in the air with wooden forks, to separate grain from chaff. A pair of oxen pull a simple wooden plough (a form unchanged for millennia) and the ploughman chants at them, in an endlessly repeated rhythm. Small caravans of donkeys or mules, accompanied by a few tattered men on foot, make the long journey to market from the Danakil depression (the lowest place in Ethiopia, and the hottest on earth), carrying blocks of salt, hacked from the depression floor. The men refresh themselves on the journey by chewing tiny bunches of wild peas – surprisingly delicious, as I discovered when they proffered me a handful, while trudging silently up the road. It was in the Danakil that the bones of 'Lucy' were found – one of the earliest hominid ancestors.

And on Lake Tana they still use papyrus boats, as they have done for thousands of years. But the boats themselves have short lives and even when frequently brought ashore to dry out they soon disintegrate, become paper. So, they are made anew every few weeks, a task that takes three or four hours.

Those endless generations of fragile lives, stretching back into the distant past, are more evocative to me than the fables of Lalibela, but this long history is under threat. The fishermen want larger boats, outboard engines, bigger nets. Soon, perhaps, there will be no more paper boats, and no more fish.

2012

A Slice of Watermelon

On a bright winter day in Bagh-e-Eram, the Garden of Paradise in Shiraz, a woman told me a story. Until six years earlier, she said, this entire region of Fars (the heart of ancient Persia) had been ruled by the Qashqai, a nomadic tribe which lived in a state of almost constant war with the nominal authorities. It was one of their tribal leaders, in the nineteenth century, who rebuilt this beautiful palace and its gardens – but in the endless upheavals that followed Eram passed through several hands until a rich merchant lost it in a game of cards. It was put up for sale. Desperate to regain his ancestral domain, the Khan of the Qashqai sacked a government customs house and used the proceeds to purchase Eram. Eventually the Shah of Iran felt powerful enough to order him into exile and confiscate his property – but paid enormous compensation for what the Khan had effectively stolen.

This was in 1967, when I was backpacking around the world, and I had to move on before learning more. But eventually I discovered that the woman's tale, though a jumble of memory and myth, contained an essential truth, that even when disarmed and dispossessed, the Qashqai paid little heed to the controls of central government. Nomadic, they moved twice a year between their summer pastures in the mountains, west of Shiraz, and their winter quarters on the Persian Gulf – men on foot and women riding donkeys, accompanied by vast flocks of sheep and goats. They lived in goat-hair tents, spoke their own language, were only nominally Islamic. The women dressed like princesses. I became determined to witness their migration.

It took me six years before I was able to return, to stay with friends who were teaching in Isfahan. I explored this wonderful city, its mosques and madrassas and bazaars, the vast central square, the Armenian quarter. But all the time, at the back of my mind, I was thinking of the Qashqai. It was September, they would now be on the move, on the long trek south.

I was told that my best chance of witnessing the migration was to find my way to a tiny village called Do Polan, up in the hills above Shahr-e Kord.

Before I left, I had a strange adventure.

I was walking down an empty street, relishing the warm autumn day and the quiet flutter of leaves, shading the pavement, when a car passed carrying a girl, alone on the back seat. To my own amazement, I whistled. It stopped and one of the rear doors opened. There was silence. I climbed in. The back of the old car was spacious, like an ancient London taxi, and the girl embraced me without a word being spoken, mouths locked, tongues entwined, hands groping. Then she told the driver to reverse until we stopped by an ornate doorway in an otherwise blank wall of tiny, buff-coloured bricks.

She led me inside, through a deep archway into a garden where elegant young people were chatting and drinking, sitting at white tables or lying decorously beside the pool, as waiters served drinks. It seemed like the memory of an Italian film, with the sound turned low.

The girl's passion, so explosive in the shadows of the car, evaporated in the sunshine of this strangely formal setting. She left my side and failed to return. Perplexed and baffled, I walked out to the street. Whenever I passed there again, the heavy door was bolted.

Sometimes I wonder if this was a dream.

The bus journey was slow, Shahr-e Kord dull and dusty, and I was met with blank stares when enquiring how to get from there to Do Polan. Eventually, in the market, I learnt that a battered truck was setting off for the village, haggled a modest fee and found myself on the front seat, squeezed between three bearded and shaggy men, as several others clambered onto the back. We headed into the hills – the road got rougher, the scenery more beautiful. When the inevitable puncture happened we all climbed down, the back wheels were chocked with rocks, and the tyre was changed for one looking even more decrepit. It got colder as we climbed higher and I was apprehensive that the sun might set before we arrived, but eventually we reached the top of a ridge and stopped beside a military guard post. Do Polan.

I just had time to enjoy the view of a gleaming green rice paddy, far below, and was raising my camera to take a picture when I was arrested. The sergeant in charge shouted at me for several minutes of mutual incomprehension, then two of his men were ordered to accompany me back to Shahr-e Kord. A local bus appeared and I was taken on board. This, it seemed, was the regular service to Do Polan, which I had been assured did not exist.

Sitting at the back, sandwiched between my guards, with chickens squawking in the luggage racks, their legs tied together, I rapidly gained the sympathy of my fellow passengers. Women dressed in colourful scarves and layers of gaudy skirts upbraided the increasingly embarrassed soldiers for treating this nice young man like a criminal. When we stopped at the first village everyone got out, and within a few minutes I found myself being led away by the local head man and seated on a low platform in the square. I was proffered a glass of sweet tea, in an elaborate silver holder, as villagers gathered round in the dusk.

These were Qashqai, nomads who had settled along the migration routes but remained true to their tribal traditions – the men wearing buff-coloured felt hats with raised flaps above the ears, the women flamboyant; faces uncovered, bright blue beads threaded on wristbands, spangles dotting their scarves. None of them felt any respect for my military escorts, who shuffled their rifles on the outskirts.

The bus stopped at another village to change a flat tyre (where once again I was treated as an honoured guest) before eventually arriving at Shahr-e Kord. My sense of delight in the absurdity of the past few hours was abruptly brought low, as I was marched to a military barracks and harangued for my crime. It seemed that I had strayed without a permit into a forbidden area and my explanations were treated with scorn. I was told that the next morning I would be escorted to a town, some way distant, to stand trial. Meanwhile I was taken to an iron bunk in a fetid dormitory of sleeping soldiers, given a thin blanket and nothing to eat, and left to a restless night of fear-filled dreams.

Woken at six, I was escorted by my guards to a bus stop. This, I realised, was my last chance. Once on the bus, on my way to stand trial, I should be done for. No-one would know my whereabouts and it seemed only too likely that I would end in jail.

I started jumping up and down, waving my arms, screaming and shouting, hoping to embarrass my guards. One of them pointed his gun at me, but I knew his heart wasn't in it and shouted even louder. A few passers-by stopped to look and moved uncertainly in our direction, at which point the soldiers gave up. Beckoning me to go with them, they decided to take me to their commander.

A long walk brought us to a quiet suburban street, where they knocked on the door of a reassuringly bourgeois house. It was still early, about seven o'clock, and there was a long pause before the door was opened by a tall man wearing pyjamas. This, it transpired, was the Colonel and to my joy he spoke fluent French. After a few minutes conversation he laughed, told my guards to leave and invited me in for breakfast.

We talked about the Qashqai. The Colonel himself was fascinated by the nomads, had been up into the mountains to follow their migration and showed me beautiful black and white photographs that he had taken there. He gave no explanation as to why it was a restricted area but offered me a pass that would allow me to return there later that day. I was too exhausted to do so.

It was a long, hot trudge from the Isfahan bus depot to the centre, along a road lined with men selling second-hand spare parts for trucks – wheels, tyres, exhausts, bits of engines, pieces of bodywork – all piled in oily confusion. The contrast with the spareness of nomadic life and the clean air of the mountains weighed me down. Tired, despondent, I looked up to see a fat man sitting on a bench, eating a large slice of watermelon. He caught my eye, gave a big grin, beckoned me over and cut me a slice. I sat beside him as we ate, juice dribbling down our chins. The melon was round as the man himself, the flesh bright pink, surprisingly cool on this hot autumn day, sweet but wonderfully refreshing. We smiled, and without a word spoken each had another slice. Suddenly my heart lifted at the simple pleasure of the moment.

Thirty years later.

A woman and her daughter are knotting a rug, squatting at a simple loom which takes up almost the entire floor of a small room in their house. The raw material is the famous wool from tribal flocks, grazing high in the mountains, and it is dyed with natural ingredients – skins of walnuts and pomegranate (brown and orange); dried euphorbia and rocket (yellow and green); madder for a wonderfully rich red, as once was used for the trousers of French legionaries. Only indigo is now an artificial dye, because the cost of the real thing is so high.

The work is intricate, wonderful to watch, but the rug that they are making is a Gabbeh, with a rich pile created by thousands of small knots, not the traditional flat-weave kilim. The computer-generated pattern has been given them by the factory to which they are subcontracted, and the rug is destined for the export market. Once collected by the factory it will be washed in dilute bleach, to give an impression of age.

The woman is a Qashqai, a member of the Sarebani clan of this vast tribe, but like most of them she is no longer nomadic. Settled in a small village, north of Shiraz, she weaves patterns without roots, for customers she never sees. But in her front room I spot a beautiful narrow kilim, of traditional tribal design (complete with the small irregularities, essential to give it life) – made for her own pleasure and use. It is bright, unbleached, and when I examine it closer I can still smell the sweet warmth of the wool. For the first time I see her smile, and make her a generous offer. Now, when I do my morning exercises, stretching on this rug, I am immediately transported to Iran, and to my first sight of the Qashqai migration.

Sheep and goats surge in a shaggy stream up the rocky track, followed by men and dogs, pack animals laden with tents and rugs, women on donkeys, brightly patterned clothes glinting through the trees. Some of the sheep break loose and a few of the women follow them on foot, each carrying a short stick but dressed as if for a wedding. The strays turn down a hill, suddenly steeper as it heads towards a road, but one woman keeps up with them, straight but fluid, flowing down the dusty slope, turquoise dress swirling round her ankles. There is no sign of hurry, yet she reaches the road in time to head off the sheep and turn them back.

The rams and some of the baggage have gone ahead in a truck, but this extended family of Qashqai still follows one of the ancient routes of the spring 'transhumance', from their winter pastures near the Gulf to the mountains west of Shiraz – a journey of hundreds of kilometres that can take them six weeks or more. Walking a short way with them, I relish the smell of the sheep's wool, from which the women weave their kilims and saddle bags, and the harsher tang of goats' hair, from which their tents are made. Their flocks also provide the main ingredients of their diet – milk, cheese, yoghurt and meat – but they eat no meat when on migration. There are quiet sounds of conversation, the clink of hooves on rocks, an occasional grunting cry to keep the flocks from straying. The women are beautiful, strong, unafraid of strangers, while the men seem more reserved, travel-worn. They all move steadily on, following a path which is hardly discernible.

It feels timeless, but vividly immediate.

Next day, further north, we come to a place called Sheikh Ali Khan – a high, wide valley which is the summer encampment site for a large group of Bakhtiari. There are graves here, a line of leafless poplars and a rushing stream, now swollen with snowmelt – beside which I spot a small frog, crouched in the sedge. Spring has come late and the Zagros mountains are white with snow. Only a few families have yet arrived. Rough drystone walls shelter the windward side of their black tents.

I follow a woman as she climbs swiftly up the slope, stooping to pick tiny wild leeks that she spots without seeming to look, but to me are invisible in the grass. At the top of the slope a cloth is covered with these leeks, drying in the pale sun. A donkey brays as I pass. The woman beckons me to enter the open tent where she sits on the ground with her family, henna-stained hands loose in her lap. Her three dark-clad daughters look curiously at me, shy but direct, while her husband, a dour grey-haired man in the traditional black skull cap and black and white striped coat worn by male Bakhtiari, avoids my glance. In front of the tent a convex metal disk used for baking bread leans against a small stone wall which shelters the embers of a fire. I have a sense of ambiguous welcome.

Tradition dictates that men determine much of importance in each tribe – setting dates for migration, arranging marriages and dowries, buying and selling their flocks – but my own impression is of wonderfully strong women. The men are grizzled when barely more than middle aged, but the women's hair remains black, glossy, thick. They express astonishment at the sight of grey-haired European women. They face strangers with a strong gaze.

Qashqai and Bakhtiari are the largest of about a dozen nomadic tribes in Iran, quite close neighbours but strikingly distinct. The women of the Qashqai, the more southerly tribe, spread gaudy skirts over the haunches of their donkeys as they ride with their flocks on migration – like a joyful parade. The

Bakhtiari wear darker clothes, have a more austere demeanour, are more reserved.

Such differences can be observed with the other, smaller tribes – each has its own character, sometimes its own language. But all share nomadic traditions that have long been under threat. Once these great tribal confederations accounted for a quarter of Iran's population – now little more than a tenth. And only about ten per cent of that number, perhaps one million in total, still undertake the twice-yearly migrations, of whom up to a hundred and fifty thousand are Qashqai and a similar number Bakhtiari.

Nomads live outside society, in a sense outside the law, though they have their own strong ethical codes. For that reason (and because they were not in any way 'modern') the Shah did his best to suppress them, blocking their access to tribal pastures. That may have been one of the reasons I had such difficulty in witnessing their migrations, back in the 1970s. The Islamic Revolution brought a more benevolent official response – for a few years teachers were sent with the tribes as they travelled, to ensure that education of their children was not neglected. But none of the nomads practise a particularly devout or orthodox version of Islam, and the present, theocratic regime regards them with suspicion.

In any case, the pressures and lures of modern society – the need for literacy, desire for consumer goods, digital culture – are sufficient in themselves to cause many to forsake the nomadic life and settle in villages and towns.

Those who still adhere to the traditional ways – migrating with their flocks, weaving kilims and saddle bags, dressing like princesses – are increasingly seen in visual terms, as picturesque, a scenario for tourists. But their way of life, almost unchanged for thousands of years, presents us with a far more profound challenge – of endurance, frugality, closeness to the rhythms of nature, light touch on the land, and a sense of relationships which extends beyond the immediate family to the clan, and then to the tribe. Rooted at the heart of this culture is a tradition of hospitality.

This tradition remains strong, even amongst those who have settled down, like the Bakhtiari of Chelgerd, a village in the hills west of Shahr-e Kord. A girl grins cheerfully at me as she mixes fresh dung with straw to make round patties, which she spreads in the sun to dry – essential fuel in a largely treeless region. It is dirty work but she is sturdy, self-assured. From behind a drystone wall three generations of women stand watching me. The black-clad grandmother and mother gaze at me boldly, like hawks, while a teenage girl, more colourfully dressed, peeks out shyly from behind her hands. A loose bundle of wild leeks is drying on the wall in front of them. Along the lane three more women are squatting in the dust, two of them with young children and the third teasing out strands of wool from a hank in her hand, spinning the thread on a simple wooden distaff. A bus stops and a man alights – close-cropped grey beard, black skullcap – and a small boy runs towards him, welcoming his father home. I smile in delight at their greetings.

The man notices, beckons. I hesitate, not wanting to intrude, but he smiles, insistent, and leads me into his house. Sitting on the floor, on machine-made carpets, I am surrounded by the family – Gasanfar Mohanat Hosini, his wife and five of their eight children. Gasanfar is an Arabic word for lion, but the man himself is a modest patriarch, evidently much loved – particularly by the cheeky youngest son who sits next to him, wearing miniature versions of the traditional black and white striped coat and Bakhtiari skullcap. An older boy is sent to fetch his English textbook, to help with translation, while their mother (quiet but smiling) uses metal snips to cut sugar lumps, as the tea is prepared. Soon I am enjoying delicious chai, thin unleavened bread and the best yoghurt I have ever eaten.

It is a moment of unexpected delight which suddenly reminds me of that time, years earlier, when I was offered a slice of watermelon on a dusty street in Isfahan.

1968/1973/2002

Palmyra, a Lament

In the Tower of Elahbel, in the Valley of Tombs, it was cool and dim, with only a shaft of sunlight slanting across the threshold. Tall pilasters crowned with fronds of acanthus (waving in a phantom breeze) framed stone shelves on both sides of the chamber. I reached into the dark recess above one of those shelves, stretching towards the fragment of a pale bowl. It was almost weightless, smooth and rounded on the outside, delicately fissured within. With a sudden shock I realised that the bowl was bone, the crown of a skull. Gently, carefully, I placed it back where I found it, deep in its slot in the wall, and made a wordless prayer for the dead.

The tower originally contained three hundred of these funerary pigeonholes, each of them designed to hold a single corpse – a condominium for the departed. One of many such towers on the edge of this ancient city, it was built two thousand years ago as a place of eternal rest for the wealthy citizens of Palmyra. Their rest was disturbed many times, for they were robbed of jewellery and other valuables, long ago – and then the archaeologists arrived and looted the sculpted portraits (which had once sealed each slot) and sent them to museums around the world. But that fragment of a skull survived through the centuries, until the tower was blown apart in August 2015, less than ten years after my visit.

Palmyra had a history of devastation, being attacked and ruined, rebuilt and shattered by earthquakes, and then abandoned to the winds of the desert, which covered much of it in sand.

It was 'rediscovered' towards the end of the seventeenth century by English merchants based in Aleppo, and a panoramic engraving of the ruins was published in the *Philosophical Transactions* of the Royal Society, in 1695. The leader of this expedition, William Halifax, described his first sight of the place, gazing down across Palmyra from an Arabic castle on a high crag to the northwest – as I did three centuries later, looking over his shoulder from the castle, with the setting sun throwing long shadows across the sand dunes, of colonnades and towers and a jumble of honey-coloured stone – a deserted city, silent, empty, breathtakingly wonderful. The next day at dawn (with a pale moon in the sky) I explored the ruins alone, and imagined I was the first for a thousand years.

Later, as the sun rose and a few boys with camels arrived, and sellers of souvenirs, the illusion faded, but the sense of time foreshortened persisted. The twelfth-century Arab walls surrounding the sanctuary of Bel seemed a barricade against imminent attack, with sections of Roman columns hastily piled on rubble from the ruins. The sanctuary itself (dedicated to a Mesopotamian god in AD 32) was later used as a church, and then as a mosque, and the pattern of its coffered ceiling (published by Robert Wood in 1753) served as a model for some of the great houses of eighteenth-century England. On fallen stones nearby, carvings of vines and leaves, crisp as if done yesterday, evoked an immediate delight in fruitful abundance, while an image of veiled women following a camel laden with a small palanquin (also heavily veiled) was resonant with mystery. On the walls of the Tomb of the Three Brothers names of the deceased were painted in red, in fluent brush strokes that resembled Japanese script. It was in fact Aramaic, a 'dead' language that I had heard spoken as a living tongue in the hill village of Maaloula, two days earlier, when I bought a couple of bottles of sweet red wine from the local priest, Father Toufic. Made from semi-dried grapes, the wine was a distant cousin of those enjoyed in Palmyra, in classical times.

And then there were the date palms.

The Roman name Palmyra, and its older name, Tadmur, hint at the palm trees that surrounded this oasis, four or five thousand years ago, and still do today. Hidden springs gave water and the dates provided sustenance for caravans carrying goods across the desert, on trade routes from the East to Rome. Palmyra acted as host and entrepôt, and levied taxes on everything that passed. It grew enormously rich, and powerful enough to defeat the Persian emperor. Then its queen, Zenobia, challenged Rome itself. She was forced to surrender in 273, taken captive and died in exile. The city declined, new caravan routes were established and the trade on which it had prospered dwindled and vanished. But the dates survived.

Carrying his nargileh (water pipe) – as he did wherever we went – our bus driver Adnan shouted for us to follow as he roared off on the pillion of a motorbike, steered by a local date farmer. The farmer's brother led us along a dusty track, between crumbling mud brick walls that bordered the patchwork of small plots which subdivided the palm groves. Eventually we arrived, to discover Adnan seated in the shade, smoking his pipe (tobacco scented with rose petals) beside a trestle table laden with sacks of dates, a few of the twenty different varieties cultivated at Palmyra. Each was named as we tasted it, and then a small boy was sent to shin up a nearby tree and cut down a bunch from the golden clusters that gleamed above our heads. These, we were told, were Ibrahim dates – lighter in colour than most, slightly less sweet, but with a delicious nutty flavour that I preferred to all the others.

I bought a bag of them, munched them throughout the rest of my time in Syria and took some home to Suffolk. The taste of these dates was what I remembered most vividly from Palmyra. That distinctive flavour, with a hint of the dry desert air, seemed a direct link to the ancient past of this city, alive, evocative, cutting through history. It was the taste of the caravanserai, when Palmyra was young.

Then came news of the catastrophes that overtook Syria, the destruction, the killings, the savagery of fanaticism and its repression. So now, when I think of Palmyra, I remember the Bedouin woman (gravely beautiful, pregnant, with two small children clutching at her skirts) who tried to sell me souvenirs at the Tomb of the Three Brothers, and our driver Adnan with his water pipe, and the date farmers. And I wonder with dread what happened to them.

And I think of the old barman at Baron's Hotel in Aleppo, and the hotel itself, almost unchanged since T. E. Lawrence shot wildfowl from the terrace – where I drank whisky, sunk in a leather armchair, dreaming of a past that I never knew. And of the family celebrating a wedding in a famous restaurant in the city, who invited me to join them and plied me with wine. And the Druze children, waving to me as I strolled through the Roman city of Shahba. And the young bakers at Deir ez-Zor, on the banks of the Euphrates, who gave me a taste of unleavened bread, blistered by the heat of the oven, late at night. And the veiled girls, graceful as gazelles, harvesting cotton stalks in a field near Halabiyeh. And the baby asleep in an improvised hammock, slung from an olive tree outside the 'dead village' of Kfer al Bara, as three generations of her family gathered the olives and piled them into sacks. And the men travelling to work in the back of a builder's truck in Damascus, who grinned as I passed, early in the morning on my first day in Syria. And Yusef the shoeshine boy, who haggled with me for quadruple his usual fee, as he polished my shoes on the pavement, on my last day.

In all that destruction, did they survive?

Who's there?

2006/2015

Daunt Books

Founded in 2010, Daunt Books Publishing grew out of Daunt Books, independent booksellers with shops in London and the south of England. We publish the finest writing in English and in translation, from literary fiction – novels and short stories – to narrative non-fiction, including essays and memoirs. Our modern classics list revives authors whose work has unjustly fallen out of print. In 2020 we launched Daunt Books Originals, an imprint for bold and inventive new writing.

www.dauntbookspublishing.co.uk